Women of Achievement

Angelina Jolie

Women *of Achievement*

Abigail Adams
Jane Addams
Susan B. Anthony
Tyra Banks
Clara Barton
Nellie Bly
Julia Child
Hillary Rodham
Clinton
Marie Curie
Ellen DeGeneres
Diana, Princess
of Wales
Amelia Earhart
Tina Fey
Ruth Bader Ginsburg

Joan of Arc
Angelina Jolie
Helen Keller
Madonna
Michelle Obama
Sandra Day O'Connor
Georgia O'Keeffe
Nancy Pelosi
Rachael Ray
Anita Roddick
Eleanor Roosevelt
Martha Stewart
Barbara Walters
Venus and Serena
Williams

Women of Achievement

Angelina Jolie

ACTRESS AND ACTIVIST

Dennis Abrams

An Infobase Learning Company

ANGELINA JOLIE

Chelsea House
An imprint of Infobase Learning
132 West 31st Street
New York, NY 10001

Library of Congress Cataloging-in-Publication Data
Abrams, Dennis, 1960–
    Angelina Jolie : activist and actress / by Dennis Abrams.
        p. cm. — (Women of achievement)
    Includes bibliographical references and index.
    ISBN 978-1-60413-909-9
    1. Jolie, Angelina, 1975– 2. Motion picture actors and actresses—United States—Biography. I. Title. II. Series.

    PN2287.J583A27 2011
    791.4302'8092—dc22
    [B]
                                        2011000035

Chelsea House books are available at special discounts when purchased in bulk quantities for businesses, associations, institutions, or sales promotions. Please call our Special Sales Department in New York at (212) 967-8800 or (800) 322-8755.

You can find Chelsea House on the World Wide Web
at http://www.infobaselearning.com.

Text design by Erik Lindstrom
Cover design by Ben Peterson and Alicia Post
Composition by EJB Publishing Services
Cover printed by Yurchak Printing, Landisville, Pa.
Book printed and bound by Yurchak Printing, Landisville, Pa.
Date printed: July 2011
Printed in the United States of America

10 9 8 7 6 5 4 3 2 1

This book is printed on acid-free paper.

All links and Web addresses were checked and verified to be correct at the time of publication. Because of the dynamic nature of the Web, some addresses and links may have changed since publication and may no longer be valid.

CONTENTS

An Eye-Opening Experience

I'm extremely honest, and I pride myself on it. I don't try to be shocking. I'm playful and know when something I'm saying is shocking, but it's just the truth. I never wanted to be scary to people or upsetting to people. I simply want to live the way I need to live.[1]

—Angelina Jolie

For Angelina Jolie, 2000 was a huge year, personally and professionally. Recently divorced from actor Jonny Lee Miller, on May 5 of that year, she married actor Billy Bob Thornton, the man she credited with teaching her to love and accept herself, saying, "We didn't belong anywhere 'til we met each other. We understand each other completely. I didn't even know how to love myself until Billy taught me what love is."[2]

7

Their marriage was the kind of relationship that tabloid headlines are made of, as stories of vials of blood worn
around each other's necks, of tattoos, of knives, of exceed-
ingly loud proclamations of love and affection stared down
shoppers standing in line at grocery stores around the country. Jolie's reputation as a Hollywood "bad girl," as a goth
princess, as a take-no-prisoners, try-anything-once, almost
dangerous, slightly scary, and threatening movie star was at
its peak.

As an actress, she was at the top of her game, having
won the Golden Globe and the Academy Award for Best
Supporting Actress for her startling performance in the
film *Girl, Interrupted*. To top it all off, she accepted the
title role in *Lara Croft: Tomb Raider*, her biggest-budget
film to date. If it was a success, it would lift Jolie from the
ranks of countless talented actresses and make her that
rarest of all commodities: an international superstar.

The film, based on the popular video game *Tomb Raider*,
would require Jolie to learn a proper British accent as well
as undergo rigorous martial arts training so that she could
properly play Lara Croft, an archaeologist, photojournal-
ist, and action hero. The accent came easily. The martial
arts training took a lot of work: Among the disciplines she
had to learn were kickboxing, yoga, and weapons training,
along with sled-dog racing and even motorbike racing. It
was quite a challenge for the skinny graduate of Beverly
Hills High School, as Jolie said in an interview from the set
of the film:

> When I first got here, I felt like this little geek, this
> scrawny, young actress from LA. I was extremely out
> of shape. I had not gone to the gym in years. And
> then through all the training, my body had changed
> and my mind had changed because I had a totally
> different focus.[3]

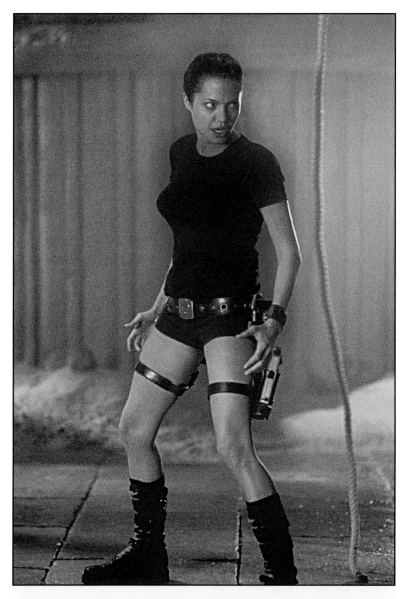

Through martial arts training, kickboxing, and even sled-dog racing, 25-year-old Angelina Jolie got into the best shape of her life while preparing to appear in *Lara Croft: Tomb Raider* in 2000. The time she spent filming *Lara Croft* in Cambodia would change her life in other ways, as well.

In many ways, for the previously fast-living Jolie, it was like waking up at the toughest boot camp imaginable, at least compared with her earlier way of life:

> I smoked a lot, drank far too much, suffered from insomnia and, like every other person I know, was imbalanced. I had to undergo a complete readjustment when I started filming. From the time I got up in the morning I had to drink a certain amount of water, had protein checks with food experts, ate egg whites and took vitamins, and all the bad things in my life were taken away.[4]

All of her hard work paid off. By the time filming was set to begin, Jolie was in the best shape of her life and had never felt or looked better. Shooting was scheduled to take place at England's Pinewood Studios, then in Iceland, and finally in China on top of the Great Wall. When skyrocketing costs and politics put an end to the possibility of the Chinese shoot, however, the location was moved to Cambodia.

There, in the jungles just 135 miles (217 kilometers) northwest of the capital city of Phnom Penh, lay the ancient ruins of Angkor Wat, one of the world's greatest archaeological treasures. This remarkable site, the twelfth-century capital and temple city of Cambodia and the nation's number-one tourist attraction, would be the perfect setting for Lara Croft's adventures. It would also be the location for a major change in Jolie's view of the world, one that would send her life in a completely different direction from her hard-living, bad-girl days.

AN EPIPHANY

For the 25-year-old Jolie, it seems likely that being in shape and healthy, and feeling good about herself, helped to open her up to what Cambodia had to offer:

She [Lara] made me feel beautiful for the first time in my life. We filmed much of the movie in Cambodia, and I was in the best physical shape of my life. I loved running through the jungle, getting very sweaty and enjoying the fact that I was playing this very physically threatening character. Since that time I've felt confident in my looks. I wake up not thinking that I'm odd-looking but that I'm beautiful.[5]

IN HER OWN WORDS

In an interview on the Web site NYRock, Angelina Jolie talked about creating the character of Lara Croft:

> I think we realized early on that because of the type of character that Lara is, you can't pretend to be her, you have to be her. Like you can't pretend to do the stunts, and wear the guns and shoot them, and just run around like that. The character has to actually do those things. And every day was this tempting obstacle course. You know, doing it as her, with the confidence of her and the fun of her. And I found, to my surprise, that I loved it. That it was in me, and I was able to keep going and wanted to keep going. I wanted to keep getting back into it, even when I hurt myself. And I was really happy when we would accomplish something. So I was really having fun.*

* Prairie Miller, "Angelina Jolie on Filling Lara Croft's Shoes and D-Size Cups." NYRock, June 2001. http://www.nyrock.com/interviews/2001/jolie_int.asp.

Working in Cambodia without the company of her husband, feeling alone and yet newly confident, Jolie was, despite the pressure of starring in a high-budget film, eager to learn more about the strange and exotic land she found herself in. Spending days working in the sacred site of Angkor Wat, complete with ever-chanting Buddhist monks, Jolie's spiritual side was awakened. And what she learned about Cambodian history and the land that surrounded Angkor Wat awakened her humanity.

She found herself moved and touched by the Cambodian people and their power of survival. For much of the previous 30 years, Cambodia had been ravaged by war. From the U.S. invasion and bombing during the Vietnam War, to the nightmarish rule of the Khmer Rouge, which resulted in the death of more than 2 million civilians, and then through years of civil war that finally ended Khmer Rouge rule, the Cambodian people, against seemingly overwhelming odds, had endured.

But even when peace finally came to their beautiful country, the scars of war were ever present, as was the constant reminder of war: Four million to six million unexploded land mines were still dispersed throughout the country. Hidden just below ground, these devices are designed to explode when a vehicle (or an unsuspecting person) makes contact with them.

It has been estimated that from 1978 to 1998, more than 40,000 Cambodians suffered amputations, the loss of a leg or an arm, because of land mines—a rate of nearly 40 people per week. In 1998 alone, more than 1,000 Cambodians died from injuries caused by land mines—many of them children who unknowingly stepped on mines on their way to school or while playing with friends. In 2000, it was estimated that, at the current rate of progress, it would take more than 100 years to clear all the land mines out of Cambodia. (Of course, Cambodia is not the only war-ravaged nation with a problem with land mines—the United Nations has reported that it will take more than 1,000 years to remove all the land mines from the world.)

Being in Cambodia deeply affected Jolie. By listening to the stories of the people she met and by learning about the nation's history, she had what she later described as an "epiphany," an experience that allowed her to see the bigger picture, to feel for herself the real world outside of Hollywood.

Jolie described her Cambodia experience in an interview with Prairie Miller for the Web site NYRock:

> Cambodia is the most beautiful place I've ever been to. I don't want to get into the heaviness of it here, but I discovered things about what's happening in the world. Like my eyes started to open. When I was in Cambodia, I learned so much about these people and what they had been through. I expected to meet a certain kind of people because of that. And when I met them, they were so generous, spiritual, and open and kind. So I couldn't believe that they would have such patience with us, and such openness after all of that. There were areas we shot in, that we could only be in certain places, because they hadn't been de-mined yet. And to know that there are hospitals where kids are still being affected by stepping on land mines every day, was horrifying and so sad. You never hear about that. To discover that kind of stuff was to really understand people in the rest of the world. So Cambodia was really eye-opening for me.[6]

Her time in Cambodia did more than open her eyes, though—it changed her life. For Jolie, just knowing that there was a problem wasn't enough—she wanted to help

Phork Roeun, who was the victim of a land mine in 1987, sits on his three-wheeled bicycle in a refugee camp in northern Cambodia in 1998. During the filming of *Lara Croft* in Cambodia, Angelina Jolie met land-mine victims and refugees and learned about the country's brutal recent history. She had what she called an "epiphany" and reached out to the Office of the United Nations High Commissioner for Refugees in an effort to help.

solve it. But what could she do? Shortly after shooting ended on *Lara Croft: Tomb Raider*, Jolie contacted the Office of the United Nations High Commissioner for Refugees (UNHCR) and volunteered her services, offering to help in any way she could. As she told UNHCR officials: "You might think I'm crazy, I'm an actress. I don't want to go with press. If you could give me access, allow me in on a trip so that I could just witness and learn."[7]

Jolie shrewdly realized that what she had to offer the UNHCR was something that all the money in the world couldn't buy—fame. She knew that her position as a movie star and a regular tabloid fixture could help her (and in turn, the UNHCR) reach out and educate people in a way that a nonfamous person never could. "If I can use this celebrity thing in a positive way, that might mean young people get involved, it has to be worth it."[8]

Within just a few months, Jolie was on her way to the war-ravaged African nation of Sierra Leone as well as to Tanzania. It would be the first of many such trips that Jolie would take, putting her own life at risk to do what she could to help fellow citizens of the world who were in need. By doing so, she has helped to educate and awaken the conscience of Americans by making them aware of the world outside their borders.

For Jolie, though, the journeys she has taken around the world are nothing compared to the personal journey she has made within herself. As Hollywood royalty, the daughter of an Academy Award-winning actor who went on to win an Oscar herself, Jolie has, in the course of her life, been a misfit, a rebel in black, a young woman who experimented with drugs and cutting, an aspiring fashion model, a gossip column favorite, a respected dramatic actress and action film hero, a mother, a fashion and beauty icon, as well as a humanitarian whose tireless efforts on behalf of children and refugees earned her the first-ever Citizen of the World Award from the United Nations Correspondents Association.

It has been a long and fascinating journey. How did she do it? How did a Hollywood bad girl become a Citizen of the World? Her story begins, naturally enough, in Los Angeles, California, with the marriage of actor Jon Voight to aspiring actress Marcheline Bertrand in 1971.

A Child of Hollywood

Jon Voight's first acting experience was as a high school junior in the musical *Song of Norway*. His performance drew raves from everyone who saw it, and even though he followed it up the next year with another strong showing in *The Student Prince*, he remained uncertain whether acting was really for him.

In college his major seemed to change yearly, switching from speech to drama to art. After completing his degree in 1960, he moved, as do so many aspiring actors, to New York City. He found success in small off-Broadway dramas and musicals and even appeared in the original Broadway production of *The Sound of Music* in the role of the Nazi love interest, Rolf, singing "Sixteen Going on Seventeen."

The attention he received as an actor in New York earned him an invitation to go to San Diego, where he starred in the 1966 National Shakespeare Festival at the Old Globe Theatre. Other roles followed in New York, including an award-winning performance opposite legendary Greek actress Irene Papas in the Frank D. Gilroy play *That Summer—That Fall*.

Voight was building a strong career in the theater, At the same time, though, other actor acquaintances of his were making it big in films and reaching much larger audiences than he could ever dream of reaching on stage. One of these was a young actor who had been the assistant director and stage manager for *A View from the Bridge*, a production in which Voight had appeared in 1965. Just two years later, that young actor, Dustin Hoffman, starred in the smash film *The Graduate*, a role that launched his more than 40-year career as an actor and movie star, during which he has collected two Academy Awards.

So when Voight heard that British director John Schlesinger was planning to direct the film version of one of his favorite novels, James Leo Herlihy's *Midnight Cowboy*, and that Hoffman had been cast in the showy role of Ratso Rizzo, he knew he had to play the lead role of Joe Buck. He was certain that the role, that of a young handsome Texan who comes to New York in the hope of making it big as a male prostitute, would make him a star.

He won the role. And as he predicted, after the film's release in 1969, Voight became a star. He (along with Hoffman) was nominated for an Academy Award for Best Actor, and while he didn't win (he lost to film legend John Wayne in *True Grit*), the film itself won three Academy Awards, including Best Picture. Voight's movie career was off to a remarkable start.

After nearly a decade toiling on stage in New York, Jon Voight (*right*) achieved movie stardom with 1969's *Midnight Cowboy*. Costarring with Voight in the groundbreaking film was Dustin Hoffman (*left*). Both Voight and Hoffman earned Academy Award nominations for Best Actor for their work in the movie.

Not only was his professional career in high gear, but his personal life was going strong as well. Blond, blue-eyed, and remarkably handsome, Voight was fairly irresistible to women. In 1971, an agent at the William Morris agency showed Voight a photograph of his girlfriend, Marcheline Bertrand (born Marcia Lynne), a popular model who was trying to become an actress.

Bertrand was attractive and exotic, with a bit of mystery. Because Bertrand's name sounds French, she was often mistaken for an actress from France, but Jolie has insisted many times that that simply wasn't true. "My mother is as far from

French Parisian as you can get. . . . She's part Iroquois Indian, from Chicago. She grew up in a bowling alley that my grandparents owned."[1] Whether Bertrand was actually Iroquois is questionable. Years later, Voight admitted that he and his wife had made up her Native American heritage to make her seem more exotic. "We always liked the idea of her as an Iroquois, and I love that my kids have picked up on that."[2]

Voight was captivated by Bertrand's looks and called her up to ask her to meet him for tea at the five-star Beverly Hills Hotel. It was only their first meeting, but he was hooked. While they began to get to know each other, the 32-year-old Voight suddenly blurted out to the 21-year-old aspiring actress that he wanted to have two children with her. "The words just came out of my mouth," he explained years later. "But she didn't blink, and neither did I."[3]

Although Voight already had a live-in girlfriend, actress Jennifer Salt, the daughter of the screenwriter of *Midnight Cowboy*, it didn't seem to matter. Bertrand had a boyfriend, actor Al Pacino, but that didn't seem to matter either. Voight and Bertrand married on December 12, 1971.

Two years later, after suffering a miscarriage a year earlier, Bertrand gave birth to a son, James Haven Voight. With that, Bertrand put her dreams of being an actress on hold, determined to be the best mother possible and to devote herself to making her kid's own potential dreams of stardom possible. Two years later, James Haven was joined by a sister, Angelina Jolie Voight, born on June 4, 1975.

The name "Angelina" came from three sources: Bertrand's grandmother, Marie Louise Angelina; a close family friend, Angelina Stogel; and the Rolling Stones' hit single "Angie." She was given the middle name "Jolie," with the dream that, when she too entered show business, she could drop the name "Voight" and be known simply as Angelina Jolie. Little did Bertrand dream that Angelina would, by the time she was 25, not only do just that, but also become the world's most popular female star in the process.

A FAMILY DIVIDED

Within one year of Angelina's birth, the Voight family was no more. In the fall of 1975, Jon Voight became the artist-in-residence for one semester at California State University, Northridge, where he would play the lead role in William Shakespeare's classic drama *Hamlet*.

While looking for a student actress to play opposite him as Ophelia, Voight saw a beautiful young woman, Stacey Pickren, appearing in the ancient Greek comedy *Lysistrata*. Once again, Voight was dumbstruck by the beauty of a young actress, and according to Jolie's biographer Andrew Morton, muttered to himself, "That is the woman I am going to spend the rest of my life with,"[4] seeming to forget that he had a wife and two young children waiting for him at home.

Voight and Pickren began a passionate love affair, and when Bertrand learned about it, she knew that her marriage was over. Voight moved out of their apartment, leaving his two children behind, and moved in with Pickren. His wife had to pick up the pieces of her life on her own. Family friend and babysitter Krisann Morel described the situation:

> Marche was so distraught about the breakup. Jon was the absolute love of her life. Every morning she would pour her heart out. "What am I going to do?" Marche would say. She was baffled, absolutely *tormented* by the affair. She couldn't get her head around why he would leave her for another woman.[5]

Growing up without a father obviously affected Angelina—how could it not? But even her father was surprised at the depth of her reaction, noting that "she was a baby when we were divorced, so it surprised me when she said it affected her as severely as it did."[6]

Voight tried to be around as much as his career and new life allowed. Although Jolie later said that "I never remember a time when I needed my father and he wasn't there"[7] and that she was "never angry"[8] with him for leaving, the truth remains that father and daughter would go on to have a sometimes loving, sometimes strained, sometimes difficult, and always complex roller-coaster relationship.

As a young girl, though, Angelina adored her father and was very much a daddy's girl. According to Voight, "When Marcheline and I broke up, I sat Angie down and asked her what kind of girl she thought her father should be with. She thought about it for a while and then said, 'Well, Daddy, maybe me, because I love you more than anything in the world.'"[9]

DID YOU KNOW?

When you're the young daughter of a movie star, it can be difficult to understand the difference between your real-life father and the roles he plays on the big screen.

In 1979, Jon Voight starred in the film *The Champ*, playing a boxer named Billy who dies from boxing injuries shortly after winning a major championship. When Angelina, who was only 4, and James, who was only 6, watched the film, they found it a disturbing experience. Angelina in particular had a hard time separating her real-life father from his character. When Billy died in the film, she thought her own father had died.

Fortunately, Voight was there to comfort her, to take her in his arms and explain to her that Daddy was only acting, he wasn't really dead, and he was very much still there with her.

It was a mutual admiration society. In an interview Voight did with Jolie in 2002, the still-doting father (the rather public split would occur the following year) described to his daughter the moment she was born:

> You don't remember it, but, when you emerged from your mother's womb, I picked you up, held you in my hand and looked at your face. You had your finger by the side of your cheek and you looked very, very wise, like my old best friend. I started to tell you how your mom and I were so happy to have you here, and that we were going to take great care of you and watch for all those signs of who you were and how we could help you achieve all that wonderful potential God gave you. I made that pledge and everyone in the room started crying. But we weren't crying; we were rapt in each other's gaze.[10]

Their time together was limited by circumstance. In 1978, Marcheline Voight, fed up with the Los Angeles smog and with still being known as "Mrs. Jon Voight," moved with her children from Beverly Hills to Palisades, New York, a quiet town just 25 miles (40 kilometers) north of New York City, to restart her career. Most of Angelina's time was spent there, with visits to and from her father as his busy schedule allowed.

Given the circumstances, her years in New York were about as normal as could be. Like many young girls, she loved to play dress-up, stomping around her house in plastic high-heel shoes. She enjoyed bouncing on her bed along with her brother to Mousercise videos. She loved the TV show *Star Trek* and one of its main characters, Mr. Spock. She loved the Walt Disney animated film *Dumbo*. She loved *Peter Pan*.

She also loved being the center of attention. She would invent acting games to play with her friends and enjoyed

Angelina Jolie sits with her father, Jon Voight, in 1978 during a party for the rock group KISS. Voight and Angelina's mother, Marcheline Bertrand, were already divorced by this time, and that year, Bertrand moved from California to Palisades, New York, with Angelina and her brother, James.

being videotaped by her brother performing in little skits, wearing costumes designed especially for her by her mother. James remembers one skit in particular, in which Angelina performed as if she were in a commercial for Subway restaurants. In it, she spoke directly to the camera, saying, "I'll punch your face if you don't buy a sandwich."[11]

Even at that young age, Angelina's aggressive streak was balanced by a need for physical affection. In elementary school, she was part of a group known as the Kissy Girls. What exactly was the aim of the Kissy Girls? As Angelina described it:

> I grew up very aware of my emotions. I was very sexual in kindergarten and I created the Kissy Girls. We would chase boys around and kiss them a lot—it involved giving them lovebites—and they would scream. Then a few of the boys stopped and started taking their clothes off and I got into trouble a lot.[12]

Young Angelina got into so much trouble, in fact, that her parents were called in to school to discuss their daughter's behavior. To no one's surprise, after that meeting, the Kissy Girls were no more.

Given Angelina's interests in dressing up, performing, and kissing boys, though, you might be surprised to learn that she could in no way be described as a "girly-girl." Instead of the standard-issue pet dog or cat, she usually had snakes and lizards—her favorite lizard was named Vladimir, and her favorite snake was named Harry Dean Stanton after the actor.

Her dream careers also provided a look at Angelina's dark side. She once announced in an interview that "while other girls wanted to be ballet dancers, I kind of wanted to be a vampire."[13] (This was, of course, years before *Twilight* and *The Vampire Diaries* made being a vampire cool.) While other girls would spend their time drawing hearts and the names of their boyfriends and such things, Angelina filled up her notebooks with drawings of old people, wide-open screaming mouths, and even barbed wire covering people's eyes.

Her dream life was soon to get even darker. Her maternal grandfather died when she was nine, and the funeral, which for most young girls would be an overwhelming and slightly scary experience, turned out to be a fascinating one for Angelina. Indeed, she found herself drawn to the very subject of death:

> My mother's father died when I was nine. He was a wonderful, spirited man, but his funeral was horrible. Everyone was hysterical. I thought funerals should be a celebration of life rather than a room full of upset people. I'm not scared of death, which makes people think I'm dark, when in fact I'm positive.[14]

Her grandfather's death affected her so strongly that almost immediately afterward, she began to dress in black and take solitary walks through graveyards. She even began to read books on the art of embalming and mortuary science to prepare herself for her dream career—funeral director. "There is something in death that is comforting," she said. "The thought that you could die tomorrow frees you to appreciate life now."[15]

Angelina was, in fact, entering a dark period of her life. It was a time when life "started not to be fun."[16] She has said of that period that "I always thought I was sane but didn't know if I'd be comfortable living in this world. As a child I contemplated suicide a lot—not because I was unhappy, but because I didn't feel useful. I had insomnia and was up all night with a mind that wouldn't stop."[17]

Unfortunately, at the same time, Bertrand decided to move the family back to California. The sensitive Angelina Jolie would be starting over again in a new school, in a new city, surrounded by all the temptations that life in Hollywood had to offer. As she once said, "Wherever I am I always find myself looking out the window wishing I was somewhere else."[18]

Looking at pictures of the beautiful, confident Angelina Jolie of today, it seems impossible to imagine her as a teenage girl, going through the same insecurities, the same attempts to figure out who she was as any other young girl. But such was the case.

When Marcheline, James, and Angelina moved back to California, they settled down in Beverly Hills. But it wasn't necessarily the Beverly Hills that one imagines from movies and television. That Beverly Hills of the rich and famous, of the zip code 90210, does indeed exist. There is another Beverly Hills, though, one not quite as rich, and not nearly as trendy. That is the Beverly Hills that the young family, getting by on Bertrand's on-again, off-again earnings, lived in, moving as necessity dictated from one basic apartment to another (Voight's income was drastically reduced during those years so his support was minimal at best.)

Young Angelina stood out from her classmates in more ways than one. While they wore the latest fashions, Angelina often came to school in ill-fitting, non-trendy clothing purchased at thrift stores. She wore eyeglasses. She had braces on her teeth. She was too skinny. Her puffy lips (a positive asset now) were the object of derision from her fellow students, who called her, among other things, "Catfish."[19]

She just couldn't fit in no matter how hard she tried (and admittedly, she didn't try all that hard). She took ballet lessons, learned to play the piano, joined the soccer team, but none of those activities were completely satisfying.

Acting in school productions *did* make her happy, which was no surprise to her father, who recalled, "She was dramatic when she was a young girl. . . . I thought maybe this gal would become an actress."[20]

So did she. So at the age of just 11, she left public school and registered at the Lee Strasberg Theatre Institute to study acting. Strasberg taught a technique popular among American actors, called "Method acting." In using the "Method," actors dig into their *own* memories and emotions to understand what the characters they are portraying are going through. Many of America's greatest actors, including Al Pacino, Robert De Niro, Paul Newman, and James Dean studied at the Strasberg Institute.

Jolie studied at Strasberg for two years, acting in several productions. While she enjoyed her time there, in many ways, she was too young to be learning the "Method." At her age, how many memories and experiences did she have to draw upon to portray the characters in the way she thought she should?

Although she didn't stay at the school, she took the lessons she learned with her. "Acting is not pretending or lying," she said years later. "It's finding a side of yourself that's the character and ignoring your other sides. And there's a side of me that wonders what's wrong with being completely honest."[21]

It would be some time, though, before she was able to apply those lessons to the craft of acting. For now she was just a teenage girl, returning to public school and life at Beverly Hills High. One of the most difficult periods of her life was about to begin.

Growing Up Hollywood

Thirteen, fourteen—that was a bad time. Yeah, very.[1]

—Angelina Jolie

It *was* a bad time. Angelina began to experiment with drugs. She began to collect knives. She began to cut herself on a regular basis. She dyed her hair purple and dressed as her mood suggested. As a friend said of her at the time: "She was into leather, torn jeans, nasty boots with stiletto heels. Kids were scared of her, the teachers were as well. I don't think there had ever been anybody quite like her at Beverly Hills High."[2]

Drugs? Knives? Cutting? What was going on?

It is an unfortunate fact of life that, for some, experimenting with drugs is part of adolescence. Oftentimes, this experimentation can spiral out of control. Angelina's interest in knives was something a bit more out of the ordinary. She said:

> I went to the Renaissance Fair when I was a little girl, and there were all these knives. There's something really beautiful about them to me. So I began collecting knives. I've collected weapons since I was a little girl.[3]

Collecting knives is one thing—cutting yourself with them is something else again. What exactly is cutting, and why does it happen? According to the Web site KidsHealth:

> Injuring yourself on purpose by making scratches or cuts on your body with a sharp object—enough to break the skin and make it bleed—is called cutting. Cutting is a type of self-injury, or SI. Most people who cut are girls, but guys self-injure, too. People who cut usually start cutting in their young teens. Some continue to cut into adulthood. People may cut themselves on their wrists, arms, legs, or bellies. Some people self-injure by burning their skin with the end of a cigarette or lighted match. . . .
>
> It can be hard to understand why people cut themselves on purpose. Cutting is a way some people try to cope with the pain of strong emotions, intense pressure, or upsetting relationship problems. They may be dealing with feelings . . . of rage, sorrow, rejection, desperation, longing, or emptiness.
>
> There are other ways to cope with difficulties. . . . But people who cut may not have developed ways to

cope. Or their coping skills may be overpowered by emotions that are too intense. When emotions don't get expressed in a healthy way, tension can build up—sometimes to a point where it seems almost unbearable. Cutting may be an attempt to relieve that extreme tension. For some, it seems like a way of feeling in control.

The urge to cut might be triggered by strong feelings the person can't express—such as anger, hurt, shame, frustration, or alienation. People who cut sometimes say they feel they don't fit in or that no one understands them. A person might cut because of losing someone close or to escape a sense of emptiness. Cutting might seem like the only way to find relief or express personal pain over relationships or rejection.[4]

Where was Angelina's mother while all this was going on? Bertrand was convinced that the best way to raise her daughter was to let her go her own way, to let her learn from her mistakes, and to be there for her when she was needed. Jolie recalled later that:

> I was raised by my mom and everything was emotional, and even if I would do something crazy, if I would be out all night and would come back, you know, at thirteen, and be doing stuff, she'd cry and then I'd feel like the worst person in the world because I hurt my friend, my girlfriend.[5]

In other words, Angelina's mother didn't treat her as a "daughter" who needed to be raised and supervised but as a friend and a shoulder to cry on.

At the same time that Angelina's fascination with drugs, knives, and cutting was in full bloom, she fell in love with her first boyfriend. Unsurprisingly, he was not the nice, clean-cut preppy who might have helped to provide balance in her life. Instead he was a 16-year-old fellow punk rocker, who happily accompanied her to Los Angeles's hottest punk music clubs.

This boyfriend also moved into Angelina's bedroom with her mother's blessing. Bertrand seemed to give her approval to this unconventional set up, believing that it would be better to have them both together where she could keep an eye on them. For most parents, letting their 14-year-old daughter live with her 16-year-old boyfriend would be unacceptable.

Years later, Angelina gave her own spirited defense for her decision to become so intimately involved at so young an age:

> Are you ever emotionally developed enough to be involved in that kind of relationship? He lived in our house with my mom and my brother, so it wasn't like we were on our own. And I could always talk to Mom if there were any problems. She was more connected and aware of what was going on than most mothers. She knew I was at the age where I was going to be looking around. Either it was going to be in weird situations or it was going to be in my house, in my room.[6]

The weird situations, though, continued in her own house, in her own room. Bored with school, she dropped out. And her relationship with her boyfriend pushed even further against the boundaries of what is acceptable, as the couple began to share a mutual love of knives, blood, and cutting. In an interview, Jolie tried to explain the appeal of such self-violence:

In April 1988, Angelina Jolie attended the sixtieth Academy Awards with her father, Jon Voight, and her brother, James Haven. Angelina's early teenage years were tumultuous, as she experimented with drugs and lived with her boyfriend in her mother's house.

Some people go shopping—I cut myself. . . . My emotions kept wanting to break out. In a moment of wanting something honest, I grabbed a knife and cut my boyfriend—and he cut me. He was a really good person, a sweet guy—not threatening, not scary. We had this exchange of something and we were covered in blood and my heart was racing and it was something dangerous. Life suddenly felt more honest. . . . It felt so primitive and honest, but then I had to deal with not telling my mother, hiding things, wearing gauze bandages to school.[7]

Things often got out of hand. One evening of knife play left a scar on Jolie's jawbone that is still evident today. On another evening when she was 16, Angelina and her boyfriend had too much to drink and the knives came out: She cut him, he cut her, there was blood, and lots of it, mainly Angelina's. One stroke of the knife came dangerously close to severing her jugular vein, requiring a trip to the hospital. It was the wake-up call she needed. "By the time I was 16, I had gotten it [cutting] all out of my system."[8]

Years later, she acknowledged that what she was going through was a desperate need to *feel*. Life in Beverly Hills did not work for her. Acting, and then her worldwide efforts on behalf of refugees and children, would do for her what experimenting with drugs and cutting did not. As she said:

I think now that if somebody would have taken me at 14 and dropped me in the middle of Asia or Africa, I would have realized how self-centered I was, and that there was real pain and real death—real things to fight for, so that I wouldn't have been fighting myself so much. I wish, when I was thinking about suicide, I'd have seen how many people are dying

each day that have no choice in the matter. I would
have appreciated the fact that I had a choice.[9]

MAKING A CHOICE

Leaving knives, cutting, and her boyfriend behind, Angelina began the process of growing up. She returned to
Beverly Hills High School, where she graduated in 1991
and, perhaps most importantly, she refocused her attention
on acting.

She began to take acting lessons from an actor who knew
his craft, her Academy Award-winning father, Jon Voight:

> She'd come over to my house, and we'd run through
> a play together, performing various parts. I saw that
> she had real talent. She loved acting. So I did my
> best to encourage her, to coach her, and to share my
> best advice with her. For a while we were doing a
> new play together every Sunday.[10]

The question, of course, is that, if Voight could be there
to help his daughter with her acting, why wasn't he around
when she was going through her difficult self-destructive
period? The answer, like most answers concerning other
people's lives, is complicated. Voight claims that he made
an effort to discipline his daughter, but because of the guilt
he felt over abandoning her and her mother, he was not
able or willing to push her as hard as he should. Indeed, in
an interview he did years later with CNN, Voight took the
blame for many of his daughter's problems:

> This was the beginning of her retaliation against
> me for the anger she felt when I left her mother.
> It was very difficult for me to scold or reprimand
> her. I backed down partially because I felt some
> guilt about the divorce and partially because I was

hoping that things would go away. It was a big mistake.[11]

But if Voight's on-again, off-again relationship with his daughter would be the cause of problems further down the line, her mother was always there for her. Jolie credited Bertrand, not her father, for her desire to become an actress. Despite her own lack of success as an actress, Bertrand turned out to be a strong teacher and manager for the aspiring actress. Jolie recalled:

> I used to work with my mom. She was the most amazing support for an actor. She used to write letters to my characters. She always read the scripts, made a bunch of notes, and wrote these letters. She was a great person to talk to about things, and she loved the process so much.[12]

An actor needs other skills besides being able to act, and Jolie set out to learn them all. To get herself into top physical shape, she learned to box at the Bodies in Motion gym in Santa Monica, California. She found a way to put her fascination with knives and swords to practical use by studying fencing at the Westside Fencing Center. And, as if to prove the seriousness of her intentions, the one-time goth princess learned to waltz, tango, and cha-cha at the Arthur Murray Dance Studio in Beverly Hills.

Through acting, through playing out scenes with her mother and her father, she was learning to express and communicate her feelings without having to resort to self-destructiveness. As she later told James Lipton, host of television's *Inside the Actors Studio*:

> There's something inside of us that we want to reach out, we want to talk to each other, we want to throw

our emotions and our feelings out and hope that we make some sense and we get an answer. The best way to do that is emote and hope that there would be a response.[13]

It wasn't her acting that first got her noticed, though. The one-time skinny, bespectacled girl had grown into her looks, ditched her glasses for contacts, and become a true one-of-a-kind beauty. She signed with the Finesse Model Management agency as a model, earning enough money working in New York, Los Angeles, and London

METHOD ACTING

When Angelina Jolie was studying acting, she learned what is known as the "Method." But what exactly is the Method?

Method acting can be loosely defined as a school of acting techniques that allow actors to create within themselves the thoughts and emotions of their characters. By doing so, it is thought that their performances have a real "lifelike" quality about them, rather than a more overblown "theatrical" quality.

The Method was first made popular in the United States by the Group Theatre in New York City in the 1930s and was brought to new levels of prominence by Lee Strasberg at the Actors Studio and the Strasberg Institute from the 1940s until his death in 1982. The Method was derived from a system created by Konstantin Stanislavski, who first originated ideas similar to these in his search for what he thought of as "theatrical truth." Stanislavski developed his system through his collaboration with Russia's greatest playwright, Anton Chekhov, and through his friendships with some of Russia's greatest actors.

to support herself while still hoping to start her career as an actress.

Acting jobs were proving hard to find. According to her own reckoning, she and Bertrand attended well over 100 auditions without getting an offer. A typical role for a young actress just starting out would be as the "girlfriend," or as "the high school girl." With her rather unconventional dark and exotic looks, however, those were not roles she was destined to play. "It was clear that my career was going to be full of very bizarre, strange women—which ended up being the ones I liked anyway," she recalled.[14]

Using Stanislavski's system, made popular in his book *An Actor Prepares*, actors were forced to take the time to analyze the motivations and emotions of their characters, so that they could portray them with psychological realism (are the character's motivations believable?) and emotional authenticity (do you believe that the emotions being portrayed are "real" or staged?).

By using the Method, an actor is told to recall emotions, sensations, or events from his or her own life and use them to find a way to identify with the character being portrayed. Of course, there are many ways to the Method—Strasberg may be its best known practitioner, but others such as Stella Adler, Robert Lewis, and Sanford Meisner all put their own spin on the Method—teaching students as varied as Marilyn Monroe and James Dean, Marlon Brando and Jane Fonda, and Angelina Jolie and Alec Baldwin—and in the process changed the art of acting in America.

Angelina Jolie poses during a portrait session in January 1991 in Los Angeles. She had signed with the Finesse Model Management agency and was getting modeling jobs in New York and London. Acting roles, though, were hard to find.

So, her first "acting" roles weren't in theater, films, or television. Music videos were at their peak of popularity, and MTV was living up to its name (Music Television) by showing videos nearly 24 hours a day. Jolie appeared in several, including those by Meat Loaf ("Rock 'n' Roll Dreams Come Through"), The Rolling Stones ("Anybody Seen My Baby"), Lenny Kravitz ("Stand By My Woman"), and Korn ("Did My Time").

These roles didn't exactly tax her acting ability. Her brother, James, who was attending the University of Southern California School of Cinematic Arts, gave her roles in five student films. While she was happy to help him with his films, the roles did nothing to advance her career.

Not willing to give up, Jolie returned to study acting at the Lee Strasberg studio and joined the Met Theatre Company. There, in her first public workshop performance, she proved to her father *and* to herself that she had what it took to become an actress.

Learning Her Craft

The play was the classic 1930s slapstick comedy *Room Service*, today best remembered from the 1938 film version staring the Marx Brothers. *Room Service*, which tells the story of a theatrical producer trying to find financial backing for his latest production while at the same time trying to avoid being evicted from his hotel room for lack of payment, features two strong female roles, played by Hollywood legends Lucille Ball and Ann Miller in the movie version.

Jolie, though, wanted to do something different. She auditioned for and won the role of Gregory Wagner, the fat, balding German hotel owner. Naturally, the part was normally played by a man. Jolie, calling on that same sense of risk taking that had ruled her life to date, played the part with strength and dominance. It was a risk guaranteed to get the audience's attention.

Sitting in that audience on opening night was her father, a man who supported her acting ambitions but had the potential to be her harshest critic. Jolie had told him nothing about what she planned to do with the role, and he was stunned to see his daughter walk out on stage as the middle-aged Wagner. When he got over his initial reaction, however, and thought about what she was doing, he recognized her bravery and audaciousness as an actress:

> I was a little shocked. But the shock came from the realization that, oh my God, she's just like me. She'll take these crazy parts and be thrilled that she can make people chuckle or whatever.[1]

To prove to herself and to her parents that she was taking her career ambitions seriously, she moved into her own place—a garage apartment just blocks from her mother's house. There, surrounded by her punk and ska CDs, her European philosophy books, and the Dostoyevsky novels *Crime and Punishment* and *The Brothers Karamazov*, she began the process that most young people her age go through—establishing their independence.

Independence didn't necessarily mean acting success, though; she was still waiting and hoping for her first big break. To date, her only major screen appearance had been a small role while still a young girl in her father's film *Lookin' to Get Out*. Voight starred as a crooked gambler; Angelina had one scene playing Tosh, the daughter of his ex-girlfriend, meeting her father for the first time. The movie, which was filmed in 1980, had trouble finding a distributor but finally opened two years later to disastrous reviews.

Fortunately for Jolie, nobody had seen the film, so she was basically starting with a clean slate as she tried to start her own film career. To further clean that slate, she had dropped the name "Voight," becoming known professionally as Angelina Jolie. And it was as Angelina Jolie in April 1992 that she faced the most difficult choice of her young career.

CAREER CROSSROADS

A major swimwear company was looking for a new face to replace supermodel Cindy Crawford, who was so big a star that she was better known than the swimwear line itself. Photographer Sean McCall, as soon as he saw Jolie's photo, knew he had found the right girl. "She was the obvious choice," he recalled.[2]

At 5-foot-7 (170 centimeters), she was considered a bit on the short side to be a top model, but she had the exotic look and beauty that McCall was seeking. With her perfect skin, her long arms and legs, and that certain indefinable "something" that made her stand out from the crowd, she seemed the ideal choice. All she had to do was prove herself in a photo audition.

She passed the test. "For her age she was the most natural girl in front of a camera I had ever seen," McCall remembered. "She was unself-conscious, whereas many teenage girls are like deer in headlights."[3] There was one interesting moment, though, that seemed to foreshadow Jolie's future: She complained about the hot studio lights, and McCall told her that, compared to movie lights, the photo shoot lights were like candles. "I would go through that for a movie,"[4] she casually responded.

The executives of the swimwear company loved the test shots, and the job seemed to be hers if she wanted it—the final hurdle would be a full-scale photo shoot at a state park in Malibu. At the last moment, though, Jolie reconsidered.

If she took the job and became the new face of the swim-wear company, it would be a full-time role. She would be a professional model with all its attendant fame and fortune, and her career worries would be over.

To do so, though, would mean putting her dreams of becoming an actress on hold for an indefinite period of time. Should she play it safe or should she roll the dice and bet that she would beat the odds and make it in Hollywood?

She took the bet and decided not to go on the photo shoot, explaining that "if that doesn't work, I will go back to modeling."[5] It was a high-risk move—as Andrew Morton points out, in the world of acting, Jolie was still a nobody. Luckily, her gamble quickly paid off. Just weeks after turning down the modeling job, Jolie was asked to audition for a big-budget science fiction film to be titled *Glass Shadow*.

By the time she auditioned, though, the film's $40 million budget had been slashed to low-budget proportions, and the title had been changed to *Cyborg 2*, technically making it the sequel to the 1989 hit film *Cyborg* starring Jean-Claude Van Damme, albeit without the presence of Van Damme. Even with the film's newly limited scope and scale, three other actresses were vying for the role of Casella "Cash" Reese, a nearly human cyborg designed to seduce and destroy.

While Jolie had had a limited career to date (all she had to show the film's producers were the student films she had made with her brother and her modeling shoots), the role was hers the moment she walked into casting. "She sucked the air out of the room, she was so gorgeous," director Michael Schroeder said. "She was special from the get-go, so talented she is a force of nature. She seemed to have the acting chops in her genes. I had a good feeling about this girl."[6]

While Jolie might have had acting chops in her genes, the role of Cash was not going to demonstrate them to

Angelina Jolie, shown here with Elias Koteas, had her first major film role in 1993's *Cyborg 2*, playing a nearly human cyborg. The movie, though, went straight to DVD, and Jolie was disappointed by the experience and her performance.

the world. In fact, the most memorable aspect of the role was that she bared her breasts, a difficult experience for the 17-year-old actress. But things were going to get even worse.

The film never played in theaters and instead went direct to DVD. Jolie was dismayed by both the film and her performance, famously stating that "when I saw it, I threw up for three days. My brother held me and I went back to school and didn't work again."[7]

Indeed, the making of and aftermath of *Cyborg 2* was so traumatic that Jolie even briefly considered taking her own life. "I didn't know if I wanted to live because I didn't know what I was living for."[8] Living on her own in New York City, away from friends and family and unhappy, she admitted that "I didn't have any close friends anymore and the city just seemed cold and sad and strange. . . . Everything that was kind of romantic about New York just got very cold for me."[9]

At one point, Jolie sat down in her hotel room and wrote a suicide note to the maid, telling her to contact the police so that the maid wouldn't have to locate the body herself. At the last minute, Jolie knew she couldn't go through with it, and instead, she went for a long walk through the streets of New York.

It was then that she saw in a store window a beautiful kimono that she decided she needed to buy, a decision that brought everything back into focus. She realized that if she killed herself, she would never get to wear the beautiful kimono that she wanted so badly, so what would be the point?

She returned to her hotel room and tore up the note, her desire for self-destruction and negation gone. "I kind of lay there with myself and thought, 'You might as well live a lot, really hard . . . because you can always walk through that door.' So I started to live as if I could die any day."[10]

This new attitude would lead Jolie to her next big film role—as well as her next important relationship.

HACKERS AND A NEW LOVE

The movie was a cyber-thriller called *Hackers*. When 15-year-old actress Katherine Heigl (who would later star in television's *Grey's Anatomy*) dropped out of the film, Jolie was asked to audition for the part. There was a lot of competition for the role: Hilary Swank, Heather Graham, and Liv Tyler were all considered, but Jolie won the part of computer whiz kid Kate "Acid Burn" Libby.

Oddly enough, given her character, Jolie was so not computer savvy that it was a point of pride for her that she still wrote exclusively in pencil. "I hate computers,"[11] she said often in interviews. For the role, though, she had to make it at least appear to audiences that she was a computer prodigy capable of helping to prevent a dangerous computer virus from being unleashed upon the world. On top of that, she had to learn another important aspect of the role—Rollerblading.

"We had three weeks of learning how to type and Rollerblade," Jolie said, "and hanging out with the cast, which was heaven—racing Jonny on Rollerblades was a big part of our relationship. We read a lot about computers and met computer hackers. With a lot of lines, I didn't know what I was talking about, but it was fascinating."[12]

"Jonny" was Jolie's costar, the British actor Jonny Lee Miller. Jolie had not had a regular boyfriend since her relationship with her punk boyfriend ended years earlier, and she was now ready to fall in love:

> We met while filming *Hackers* and I always fall in love while I'm working on a film. It's such an intense thing, being absorbed into the world of a movie. It's like discovering you have a fatal illness, with only a short time to live. So you live and love twice as deep.[13]

While her relationship with Miller thrived, the film was another critical and box-office disappointment. Although Jolie might have suspected as much when she took the role, she knew that, as an aspiring young actress, she could not afford to turn down parts. Truth be told, she was almost relieved that the movie had not reached a large audience: She didn't have to worry about being remembered for her work in this movie or being typecast in similar roles in the future.

After the filming of *Hackers* was over, Jolie tried to break off her relationship with Miller, telling him that caring about him so deeply made her feel sad and that it would be best if he forgot about her. Miller, though, was deeply in love with Jolie and was not going to give up that easily.

He has admitted doing whatever he could to make her his, that he "chased [Angelina] all over the world. I chased her all over North America until she succumbed. It took a while—a good few thousand miles."[14] Jolie made three movies (*Mojave Moon*, *Love Is All There Is*, and *Foxfire*) in quick succession after *Hackers*, so not only did Miller have Jolie's busy schedule to contend with, he also faced a challenge from her predilection to falling in love while making films. Miller's competition, however, came from an unexpected direction.

The movie was *Foxfire*. Based on a novel by American writer Joyce Carol Oates, the film tells the story of a group of schoolgirls who bond while taking revenge on a teacher who sexually harasses them. While filming in Portland, Oregon, Jolie grew very close to one of her costars, Jenny Shimizu, a Japanese-American model turned actress best known for appearing in advertisements for the Calvin Klein fragrance CK One.

It was an immediate attraction. Jolie said of meeting Shimizu, "I fell in love with her the first second I saw her. . . . I realized that I was looking at her in a way I look at men. It never crossed my mind that one day I was going to experiment with a woman. I just happened to fall for a girl."[15] Shimizu returned Jolie's feelings, complicating her already complicated relationship with Miller.

Jolie and Miller were reunited during the publicity tour for the release of *Hackers* in September 1995, giving Miller the opportunity to press his case with Jolie. Whatever he did seemed to have worked. Just six months after the film was released, she eloped with Miller. He was 23 years old; she was a few months short of her twenty-first birthday. The ceremony was so small and such a closely held secret (there were only two guests) that not even Jolie's father knew about it.

The nontraditional couple married in extremely non-traditional clothing: Miller was dressed in leather, Jolie in a white shirt and black rubber pants, her husband's name boldly written in her own blood across the back of a dazzling white shirt. To commemorate the occasion, the couple both got tattoos: Miller already had a pet snake, so he had a snake tattooed around his wrist. Jolie had a tattoo representing bravery drawn on her arms and one representing death on her shoulder. They would be the first of many to come.

Despite her love for Miller, Jolie had doubts about committing to a marriage. She knew herself, and knew that being a child of divorce gave her a strong desire to remain in control and independent. She said:

> I don't know if my childhood was any worse than anyone else's, but it is disturbing and sad when you see one parent figure not respecting the other. That probably had a great effect on me wanting to be self-sufficient. I was raised feeling that I didn't want the ground to be taken away from me, and so by the age of 14, I was already working [as a model]. I didn't want to ask for help from anybody, and that extended into my own marriages.[16]

In 1995, Angelina Jolie appeared in the cyber-thriller *Hackers* and became involved with her costar, the British actor Jonny Lee Miller, pictured with Jolie. Despite her attempts to break it off, the relationship continued after the movie was completed, and in 1996, the couple married.

On top of that, her commitment to her career would leave little time for a relationship of any kind, much less a marriage. She has said that "it's not fair to the other person that I'm so busy with my career and that I'm so often distant even when I am with someone," adding that when it came to her marriage, "We were living side by side, but we had separate lives."[17]

Despite her emphasis on her career, the right roles in the right films still weren't coming her way. In 1997, she had a part in *Playing God*, a dark comedy of drugs, gangsters, and a good doctor gone bad. The film costarred David Duchovny, whose career was soaring on the reputation of TV's *The X-Files*, and Academy Award-winning actor Timothy Hutton, and newspaper columnists quickly began to speculate about a possible relationship between Jolie and either one or both of her handsome leading men. While still not a full-fledged star, her off-screen life was winning her attention and notoriety.

That notoriety, though, didn't translate into box-office success, and *Playing God* became yet another Jolie film to receive little attention from the public and negative notices from the critics. One reviewer, Edward Guthmann of the *San Francisco Chronicle*, blatantly said that the movie was "a piece of garbage,"[18] while another even criticized Jolie's looks, calling her "sultry, dark-eyed [and] fat-lipped."[19]

It was time for Jolie to reassess her career and what she wanted from it. Feature films weren't giving her the roles she needed to prove to the world that she wasn't just another child of Hollywood, still better known for her wild ways than for her acting abilities. So, taking a calculated gamble, she moved away from the big screen to the small screen. Would the risk pay off? Or would it be a move that doomed her career before it even really started?

Critical Acclaim

Angelina Jolie's first foray into television was a CBS miniseries, *True Women*, which aired in May 1997. It starred Dana Delany as Sarah McClure, with Annabeth Gish as Euphemia Ashby and Jolie as Georgia Virginia Lawshe Woods, three pioneer women struggling to survive in nineteenth-century Texas.

The show was only a moderate success, but it was what occurred during the filming of the miniseries that led to Jolie's breakthrough as an actress. A TV movie was being made that would tell the life story of George Wallace, the controversial governor of Alabama who, in the 1960s, had led his state in the fight against equal rights for African Americans.

(continues on page 54)

GEORGE WALLACE

In the 1997 television film *George Wallace*, Angelina Jolie earned her reputation as a serious actor with her performance as Wallace's second wife, the former Cornelia Ellis Snively (1939–2009).

George Corley Wallace Jr. (August 25, 1919–September 13, 1998) was the forty-fifth governor of Alabama. A four-time candidate for president of the United States, he was left paralyzed and wheelchair-bound for the rest of his life after a 1972 assassination attempt. He is best remembered today, however, for his pro-segregation stances taken during the period of American desegregation, positions that he renounced later in life.

Before the civil rights movement, Alabama (as well as other Southern states) had strong segregation laws in effect, laws designed to keep African Americans separated from the rest of society. There were public schools for whites and public schools for African Americans. There were restaurants for whites and restaurants for blacks. There were even drinking fountains for whites and drinking fountains for African Americans.

Times were changing, though, and the combination of a series of decisions from the United States Supreme Court, laws passed by Congress, and shifting public opinion began the slow process of tearing down the laws that led to segregation—a process known as desegregation. Governor Wallace, however, made the decision to defy federal laws protecting the rights of African Americans and to defend the state laws that had separated whites and African Americans for 100 years.

He made headlines when, in his inaugural speech after being elected governor, given on January 14, 1963, he said:

In the name of the greatest people that have ever trod
this earth, I draw the line in the dust and toss the gauntlet
before the feet of tyranny, and I say segregation today,
segregation tomorrow, segregation forever.*

It was a losing battle but one that made him a hero in the
eyes of many. He stood in the doorway of Foster Auditorium
at the University of Alabama on June 11, 1963, in an attempt
to stop the enrollment of the school's first African-American
students, Vivian Malone and James Hood. He tried to stop four
black students from enrolling in four elementary schools in
Huntsville, Alabama, in September 1963. In both cases, he was
forced to back down and ultimately allow the enrollments to
take place.

He ran for president four times and failed but served four
terms as governor of Alabama. Throughout his career, he maintained his opposition to integration, but in the late 1970s,
after years of pain and suffering following the failed assassination attempt, he announced that he had become a born-again
Christian and apologized to black civil rights leaders for his
earlier views. Whether his change of heart was real or merely an
attempt to salvage his reputation in a world that had very much
changed is still a matter of debate. He died on November 13,
1998, from respiratory problems in addition to ongoing complications from the gunshot injury to his spine.

* "The 1963 Inaugural Address of Govenor George C. Wallace,"
Alabama Department of Archives and History. http://www.
archives.alabama.gov/govs_list/inauguralspeech.html.

(continued from page 51)

Jolie was asked to try out for the role of the governor's second wife, Cornelia, a slightly outrageous, sexy, very Southern woman. The director was John Frankenheimer, the man behind such Hollywood classics as *The Manchurian Candidate* and *Birdman of Alcatraz*. Jolie was visibly nervous when auditioning for him, the most important director she would have ever worked with, and so to help ease her nerves, Frankenheimer asked her, "So Jon's your father. How's he doing, and what's he up to?"[1]

That was *exactly* the wrong question to ask Jolie, who wanted to be known for herself, not for her famous father. As she later confessed to *Back Stage* magazine, "My heart just sank, and I thought, 'He didn't pay attention to anything I just did.'"[2] Without thinking about it, Jolie snapped at Frankenheimer, saying that, if he was that concerned about her father's health, he should call him himself, and stormed out of the audition.

Minutes later Jolie's manager, Geyer Kosinski, was on the phone with his willful client, scolding her for leaving the audition and urging her to try again. Her second audition was a triumph, and the role was hers. She had landed the part that would change her life and her career. As biographer Andrew Morton pointed out, no longer would people talk about her in terms of the men in her life; by playing Cornelia Wallace, they would talk about her as an actress.

The three-hour film traced the career of George Wallace from racist politician to his final years, paralyzed in a wheelchair from a failed assassination attempt, begging for forgiveness for his past sins against the African-American community. It was Cornelia Wallace, best remembered by the American public from the famous photo of her shielding her husband's body after the assassination attempt, who was with him on his attempted road to redemption. It was

Dismayed by the types of roles she was getting in feature films, Angelina Jolie turned to television. In 1997, she appeared in *George Wallace*, a three-hour TV movie about the life of the controversial Alabama governor. She portrayed his second wife, Cornelia, while Gary Sinise played Wallace.

that image of Cornelia Wallace that helped to inspire Jolie's performance, portraying her as a strong woman who loved and supported her husband at any cost.

For Jolie, making the movie, the most important of her career, changed her entire attitude toward film and acting, saying, "For the first time I saw the grand scale of what you can attempt and what you can achieve."[3] The movie was a huge success, earning multiple Golden Globe and Emmy nominations and winning Jolie the first major award of her career: the Golden Globe for Best Supporting Actress in a Series, Miniseries, or Motion Picture Made for Television.

Accepting the award, Jolie thanked her director John Frankenheimer for being "brilliant"[4] and credited him and the entire production staff for helping to restore her faith in acting. "*Wallace* was the first thing I did where I felt their ideas were better than mine."[5] Frankenheimer returned the favor, saying, "The world is full of beautiful girls. . . . But they're not Angelina Jolie. She's fun, honest, intelligent, gorgeous, and divinely talented."[6]

If *George Wallace* would prove to Jolie and the world that she was more than just a beautiful face with a famous father, that she could give a performance of meaning and depth, her next role would test her to the fullest, pushing her talent and her emotional state to the breaking point.

GIA

The film was called *Gia*. It was, like *George Wallace*, a "biopic," a film that tells the story of a real-life person, in this case the drug-addicted supermodel Gia Marie Carangi. Born on January 29, 1960, Carangi reigned as one of the first-ever supermodels in the late 1970s and early 1980s, and her life was one of great success and, at its end, great tragedy.

Her rise to superstardom, from her obscurity off the streets of working-class Philadelphia, was rapid, and Gia, like many overnight celebrities, succumbed to the pressures of fame and fortune. She turned to drugs and would often show up at photo shoots heavily under the influence of heroin. Her addiction became so bad that, by the time of her last photo shoot in 1982, she had to hold her hands behind her back to hide the scars left on her arms from near constant heroin injections.

She tried rehab on several occasions, fell in and out of love, mostly with women, and, with her career over, spiraled downward into prostitution, before dying of AIDS-related complications on November 18, 1986, at the age of just 26.

The role was a deeply challenging one, one that would test Jolie's acting abilities to the utmost. She hesitated about accepting the part, turning it down four times before deciding to take the role. Once she did, however, she dedicated herself to it 100 percent, to the point of placing her own emotional health and her marriage at risk.

She knew that taking the role and using everything she learned about the "Method" meant accessing the darkest parts within herself. "Gia has enough similarities to me that I figured this would either be a purge of all my demons or it was really going to mess with me," said Jolie.[7] The similarities between Gia and Angelina were uncanny: They had both felt like outsiders growing up. They had both experimented with their sexuality. They had both been models and both had to deal with being judged solely on their looks. And, perhaps most importantly, they had both used drugs. While Jolie's experiences with drugs were probably nowhere close to Gia's, they were still enough to give her a powerful insight into the supermodel's character.

Jolie admitted that she and Gia had much in common, saying, "She was a lot like me, although the key to her was she needed to be loved. I want to be understood. Maybe that's the same. She was a good person who self-destructed when things went bad."[8] Using the tools she had learned from the Strasberg Institute, she dug deep into herself and became completely immersed in the character, cutting herself off from family and friends in an attempt to actually *become* Gia Marie Carangi during filming.

It was an act of extreme personal and artistic bravery—a total devotion to the role and to her craft. At one point, for example, she told her husband as she steeped herself in the part, "I'm alone, I'm dying, I'm gay; I'm not going to see you for weeks."[9] The film's director, Michael Cristofer, had nothing but praise for the dedication and hunger Jolie brought to the role, saying:

She's a hunter. I think most of us are cowards; we live at home in our nice little worlds, and the artists are the ones who come along, the adventurers, who go out into the dark away from the campfire and then they come back and tell us the story of their adventures. She's one of those people. Life is an adventure for her.[10]

Jolie has always been one to share the adventure with her fans. She *wants* them to know what her life has been like, what she has gone through, to know her weaknesses and her strengths. She's aware of the tendency of people to assume that those in the spotlight, who always appear in public without a hair out of place, always looking perfect, are perfect. But by revealing parts of herself in her work, as in her portrayal of Gia, she presents another side. As Jolie said in an interview:

Wouldn't it be more helpful for a young girl to know of the things I've discovered, the mistakes I've made, of how human I am, and how like her I am? That's more interesting than, "Here is how much stuff she has and how fabulous her life is."[11]

Her performance in *Gia* cemented her reputation as one of America's finest and bravest young actresses. Will Cooper of the *Daily News* in New York wrote, "Hers is the real art behind this artifice and her fire is what makes HBO's *Gia* burn so brightly."[12] *Variety* described her performance as "a mesmerizing tour de force,"[13] and Lee Winfrey of the *Philadelphia Inquirer* raved, "If you like to see the birth of a star, watch *Gia*."[14]

Jolie was amply rewarded for her work, winning a Golden Globe for Best Actress in a Mini-Series or TV Film and a Screen Actors Guild Award for Best Female

Angelina Jolie's bravura performance as the troubled supermodel Gia Marie Carangi in the 1998 HBO biopic *Gia* secured her reputation as one of the era's finest young actresses. She won a Golden Globe and a Screen Actors Guild Award for her portrayal.

Actor in a TV Movie or Miniseries. But her extraordinary effort, dedication, and bravery in achieving that performance took its toll. After the filming of *Gia* was complete, she felt empty, physically and emotionally exhausted. "I felt like I'd given everything I had, and I couldn't imagine what else was in me."[15]

She was certain that she was going to give up acting, and, sinking into a period of depression, she again contemplated ending her own life. This time, however, she had no intention of doing it herself. As hard as it may be to believe, she came close to hiring a hit man to do the job for her.

This is going to sound insane, but there was a time I was going to hire someone to kill me. The person spoke very sweetly to me, he made me think about it for a month. And, after a month, other things changed in my life and I was surviving again.[16]

Two events made Jolie change her mind. For one thing, the reviews for *Gia* had come out, and Jolie was thrilled to be accepted and to feel as though her abilities and hard work had been appreciated. "Suddenly it seemed like people understood me. I thought my life was completely meaningless and that I would never be able to communicate anything and that there was nobody who understood . . . and then I realized that I wasn't alone. Somehow life changed."[17] The other thing that changed was Jolie's ability to manage her emotions: She learned to play the drums and was able to use them to release the anger and furies that still existed within her.

After finishing *Gia*, Jolie moved to New York City to take classes at New York University's film school. The classes were in directing and writing screenplays, but she soon realized that at heart she was an actress. She returned to Los Angeles where, hot off the success of *George Wallace* and *Gia*, she appeared in five films in just a little more than a year.

Two of those were released in 1998. The first was *Hell's Kitchen*, a crime drama about a bank robbery gone wrong.

This was a little independent film, seen by few. By contrast, her second 1998 release, *Playing by Heart*, was a big-budget studio picture, an ensemble film that looked at the lives of 11 people and how they approached relationships and love.

In a cast featuring major stars like Sean Connery, Ellen Burstyn, Gena Rowlands, and Dennis Quaid, Jolie's performance was the attention-getter. One review simply put it, "Angelina Jolie, who gives the film's standout performance, is luminous."[18] The National Board of Review cited her work in the film as the Best Breakthrough Performance by an Actress.

While her career was quickly taking off, her marriage to Jonny Lee Miller was falling apart. Jolie was dedicated to her career, and Miller, an actor himself, was not willing to play a supporting role in her life. In the winter of 1999, Miller moved back to London. By the spring of 2000, the two were divorced, although they have remained good friends ever since.

Jolie blamed herself for the failed marriage; so many hours spent working on the set meant little to no time to make the relationship work. She would have little time to grieve over her divorce—on the set of her next film, *Pushing Tin*, she would meet the man who would become her second husband.

MEETING BILLY BOB

Pushing Tin was another ensemble movie, a comedy-drama about the personal and professional lives of air-traffic controllers. Jolie's role was that of Mary Bell, the wife of an air traffic controller played by actor and Academy Award-winning screenwriter Billy Bob Thornton.

Thornton and Jolie shared the same manager, Geyer Kosinski. Indeed, Kosinski at one point had told Thornton, "There's this girl, and she's kind of like you as an actor. She's the female you. I'm afraid to introduce you because I'm afraid you'll get married."[19] Of course, as it turned out, the two actors had much more in common than a manager.

They could both be fairly accused of being eccentrics, of sharing what many people would consider to be odd behavior. There was Jolie and her fascination with blood and knives. Then there was Thornton, renowned for having a number of strange phobias, including Komodo dragons, French antique furniture, silver cutlery, velvet, and even harpsichords.

Filming for *Pushing Tin* took place in Toronto, Ontario. One day, the two, who had yet to meet, got into the same elevator. Thornton introduced himself to Jolie by simply saying, "I'm Billy Bob—how are you doing?"[20] Thornton later confessed that, despite his confident approach, he was somewhat awestruck by Jolie. He said, "And then we came out of the elevator, and I just remember . . . you know wanting something to not go away? Wishing the elevator had gone to China. It's like a bolt of lightning. Something different that's never happened before."[21]

Leaving the hotel and climbing into a van, Thornton told Jolie he was going clothes shopping and asked if she'd like to come along. Without even thinking, Jolie quickly replied, "No." After the van drove away, Jolie walked around a corner and sat down, leaning against a wall. She later remembered, "I was just confused. I became a complete idiot."[22]

Although the two had an obvious connection, the timing was off—Thornton was living with and engaged to actress Laura Dern. The connection, though, could not be denied. Several months after filming ended, the pair began to talk on the phone. Jolie found that she could not stop thinking about Thornton, and she even had the name "Billy Bob" tattooed on her left arm. Not surprisingly, the two began to see each other regularly, but largely outside the glare of tabloid publicity.

While they kept their relationship hidden, films starring Jolie kept her name on movie marquees across the country. In 1999's *The Bone Collector*, Jolie played a forensic officer who teams up with a quadriplegic police detective (played by one of Jolie's acting heroes, Denzel Washington) to track down a serial killer. The role presented the ambitious actress with challenges she had never faced before: She had to confront a corpse covered with rats, as well as jump into New York City's East River fully clothed. "I wasn't sure I could play her, but that was perfect because she's not sure she can do her job either,"[23] she explained.

The film was a huge box-office success but a critical failure, and did little for Jolie's critical reputation. Her next film would be the one that would establish her once and for all as a movie talent to be reckoned with, and it would win her Hollywood's top award.

GIRL, INTERRUPTED

In 1967, after a failed suicide attempt, 18-year-old Susanna Kaysen was admitted to McLean Hospital in Belmont, Massachusetts. Diagnosed with borderline personality disorder, she spent 18 months in the hospital, becoming friends with several other patients, before being released. Twenty-six years later, Kaysen wrote a best-selling memoir describing her experiences, titled *Girl, Interrupted*.

Not surprisingly, Jolie, given her own history of suicidal thoughts, was a huge fan of the book. For her, one character in particular stood out—Kaysen's fellow patient Lisa Rowe. Rowe, labeled a sociopath, is the book's most troubled and rebellious character, and Jolie "loved her and identified with her."[24] Years later, when she found out that film star Winona Ryder, who had had her own problems with depression, was trying to get the film made, she knew she would do anything necessary to get the role.

Learning that James Mangold was slated to be the film's director, she contacted him directly and begged to be given the role of Lisa. Her pleading turned out to be totally unnecessary—once Mangold saw her audition, he knew he had found his Lisa. "She sat down, and she was Lisa. I felt like the luckiest guy on earth. Her power is volcanic, it's huge, it's electric."[25]

Many critics felt her power in the film was extraordinary. As Andrew Morton described it in his biography of Jolie:

> She stole every scene in which she appeared, experienced actors like Vanessa Redgrave and Whoopi Goldberg expertly mugged by this feral force of nature. Even the animals were upstaged. In one scene, when she was faced with a hissing cat, instead of flinching or swiping it away, Jolie calmly gave it the once-over, stared it down, and then hissed right back.[26]

As the film's executive producer, Winona Ryder had hoped that *Girl, Interrupted* would showcase her own talents, but against the sheer force that was Jolie, she and the other actresses never stood a chance. As legendary film critic Pauline Kael later said, "Those poor actresses. She's absolutely fearless in front of a camera."[27]

Her performance was impossible to ignore. She won numerous awards, including a Golden Globe for Best Supporting Actress in a Motion Picture, the Screen Actors Guild Award for Outstanding Performance by a Female Actor in a Supporting Role in a Motion Picture, the Broadcast Film Critics Association Award for Best Supporting Actress, and finally, a nomination for the big one—the Academy Award. Jolie's was the only major nomination for *Girl, Interrupted*, and Ryder's fine performance was ignored.

An overwhelmed Angelina Jolie delivers her acceptance speech after winning an Academy Award for Best Supporting Actress on March 26, 2000, for her role in *Girl, Interrupted*. "She's absolutely fearless in front of a camera," film critic Pauline Kael wrote about Jolie's performance.

The other actresses nominated for the Best Supporting Actress Oscar that year all gave sterling performances: Catherine Keener in *Being John Malkovich*, Chloë Sevigny in *Boys Don't Cry*, Toni Collette in *The Sixth Sense*, and Samantha Morton in *Sweet and Lowdown*. Yet, on the night of Sunday, March 26, 2000, it was Angelina Jolie who received the award, raising her to the level of Hollywood elite.

Dressed in her finest goth style, Jolie appeared to be genuinely overwhelmed and surprised by the award given to her by her peers in the film community. In her speech, she thanked her cast, her mother, and her father, who had won his own Oscar 21 years earlier (for *Coming Home*): "And my dad, you're a great actor, but you're a better father."[28] She ended with a proclamation of her love for her brother, Jamie, "I have nothing without you. You're the most amazing man I've ever known, and I love you."[29] With that, the usually stoic Jolie burst into tears before leaving the stage.

It was just the beginning of one of the biggest years of Jolie's life. A month later, her divorce from Jonny Lee Miller was finalized. Then, in a move that surprised nearly everyone, on May 5, Billy Bob Thornton, 44 years old and four times married, and Angelina Jolie, 24 years old and once married, were united in marriage in a Las Vegas wedding chapel.

The wedding was casual to say the least: Jolie was wearing a blue sleeveless sweater and jeans; Thornton was in jeans and a baseball cap. She carried a bouquet of red and white roses. The ceremony, the "Beginning Package" offered by the Little Church of the West Wedding Chapel, cost a grand total of $189.

None of Jolie's family was present. None of Thornton's family was there, either. Sadly, actress Laura Dern, who had expected to marry Thornton herself, only learned from a tabloid reporter that her fiancé had left her for another woman. "I went to work one morning, and he ran off and married Angelina Jolie," she told friends.[30]

Even Jolie's father was surprised by the news that his daughter had married a man he had yet to meet. When asked to comment on his daughter's new husband, he seemed somewhat hesitant to commit. "They stick by each other and care deeply for each other. You're always going through things with young people and hoping they'll come out the other side. Hopefully she'll not do anything she can't recover from."[31]

In hindsight, Voight was right to have reservations about his daughter's decision. She was about to enter one of the most public and tumultuous periods of her life. When she came out the other side, she would be a new woman.

Angelina
Discovers
the World

The marriage between Angelina Jolie and Billy Bob Thornton was featured in magazines, newspapers, and tabloids worldwide. The couple made news for their continuous proclamations of their love for each other, their public displays of affection, and, most of all, the somewhat eccentric ways in which they demonstrated their feelings.

There were the mutual tattoos: Thornton had the word "Angelina" tattooed on his left arm, with the letter 'L' wrapped around a vein. He then had four drops of blood tattooed on (made to look as though they were coming from the vein itself)—to represent him, Angelina, and his two sons from his previous marriages. The couple also had mysterious lettering tattooed on their inner right forearms.

"It means something to us, but nobody else [can know] what it means or it breaks the spell," Thornton said.[1]

But when people think about the Jolie-Thornton marriage, one image always comes to mind—the rumored vials of blood worn around their necks. It was an attention-getting, controversial gesture of love to say the least. In interviews, Jolie did her best to defend their behavior:

> Some people think a diamond is really pretty. My husband's blood is the most beautiful thing in the world to me. There are only so many ways to say you love somebody, to say, "I would truly die for you. I want to live out my days, my life with you. I am your partner, your blood, and we share the same life." It's not dark or trying to be provocative in any way.[2]

It might not have been meant to be provocative, but it certainly got the public's attention. After her film *Gone in 60 Seconds* opened to terrible reviews (although with huge box office results) as did *Lara Croft: Tomb Raider*, Jolie's reputation as an actress was being overshadowed by her new role as a popular box-office star.

As we have seen, Jolie very much enjoyed taking on the physical challenge of playing Lara Croft. While critics disliked the film, they appreciated her efforts. Critic Jack Garner of the *Rochester Democrat and Chronicle* wrote:

> Jolie also handles the role's considerable physical demands with aplomb. Whether she's bouncing from the ceiling on bungee cords or diving off a dam or coming at you with two guns blazing or zooming by on a motorcycle, she makes us believe she does it every day. She's so absolutely right for the role—it's impossible to conceive anyone else doing it.[3]

With their mutual tattoos and their repeated declarations of love for one another, Angelina Jolie and Billy Bob Thornton commanded tabloid attention. The couple, seen here at the June 2000 premiere of *Gone in 60 Seconds*, supposedly wore vials containing each other's blood around their necks.

Besides the physical training she went through and the exaltation she felt at becoming fit and strong, there were two other elements that made filming *Lara Croft* important to her. One was that, through her suggestion, her father, Jon Voight, played Lara Croft's father, Lord Richard Croft, in the film. It was the first time the two had worked together since 1982's *Lookin' to Get Out*, and the experience was a moving one for father and daughter.

The other element, of course, was her introduction to the people of Cambodia and their history. It was a first step in Jolie's education, the first step in moving outside of herself and her career and into the world. For many, it would be enough just to pay lip service to public service, to donate some money, perhaps appear in an ad proclaiming one's devotion to the world's needy, but for the newly awakened Jolie, that wouldn't be enough.

After the filming of *Lara Croft* was completed and Jolie was safely home in California, she contacted the United Nations High Commissioner for Refugees. The agency was willing to send her on a goodwill trip to one of the world's most troubled regions. She would not be returning to Cambodia, though. The UNHCR instead wanted to send her to the African countries Sierra Leone, which had suffered through a decade-long civil war, and Tanzania, one of the world's top refugee-sheltering nations. Jolie jumped at the opportunity.

For many of her friends and family, it seemed a risky and foolhardy adventure. Her father was particularly concerned and tried to get her not to go, even going so far as to contact the United Nations to get it to cancel the trip. Jolie later wrote, "I was angry with him, but I told him I know he loves me and that as my father he was trying to protect me from harm. We embraced and smiled at one another."[4]

Her husband shared her father's views, believing that she could help to publicize the problems of land mines and refugees by making donations from the comfort of her home. "Why are you doing these things? What do you think you can possibly accomplish?"[5] he asked her. Ultimately, though, he let her go ahead on the trip. "He said he didn't think I'd be safe. But he didn't offer to come along, either. And so I left,"[6] Jolie recalled.

Perhaps not surprisingly, her strongest ally in her quest came from her always supportive brother, who sent her a message through Marcheline, alluding to their favorite childhood character Peter Pan, saying, "Tell Angie I love her and to remember that if she is ever scared, sad, or angry—look up

UNITED NATIONS HIGH COMMISSIONER FOR REFUGEES

The Office of the United Nations High Commissioner for Refugees (UNHCR), established on December 14, 1950, is also known as The UN Refugee Agency. It exists as an agency of the United Nations, mandated to protect and support refugees either at the request of a government or of the United Nations itself. The agency assists in integrating refugees into their new homes, resettling them to another country, or returning them voluntarily to their homeland. Its headquarters are in Geneva, Switzerland, and it has twice won the Nobel Peace Prize—in 1954 and 1981.

According to the agency, UNHCR's mandate is to provide, on a nonpolitical and humanitarian basis, international protection to refugees and to seek permanent solutions for them.

While it was originally thought that the agency's work would largely be among European refugees from World War II, it soon became clear that the refugee problem was growing worldwide. In 1956, for example, the UNHCR was called in to coordinate the response to the Hungarian uprising; one year later, it was called in to deal with Chinese refugees in Hong in the night sky, find the second star on the right, and follow it straight on till morning."[7] Armed with nothing more than her pens, a notepad, and her brother's love and support, the Academy Award-winning actress set off to a region that some of the world's toughest reporters were afraid to visit.

HER FIRST TRIP

> I am on a plane to Africa. I will have a two-hour layover in the Paris airport, and then on to Abidjan in Cote d'Ivoire (Ivory Coast).

Kong, as well as Algerian refugees who had fled to Morocco and Tunisia to escape the turmoil of Algeria's war for independence from France.

In the 1960s, as African nations shifted from being European colonies to independent nations, large movements of refugees within Africa transformed the UNHCR. Unlike the refugee crises in Europe, there seemed to be no permanent solutions to the problems of Africa as refugees who fled one country found instability in their new country of asylum. By the end of the decade, nearly two-thirds of the UNHCR's budget was focused on operations in Africa.

As the decades progressed and new crises erupted worldwide, so too did the responsibilities of the UNHCR. In the 1970s, for example, as Bangladesh strove for independence and millions of refugees fled to India, the UNHCR was there. Today, the UNHCR has major missions in Lebanon, Sudan, Chad, the Democratic Republic of Congo, Iraq, Afghanistan, and Kenya. Indeed, as of January 1, 2007, more than 21 million people were living under the mandate of the UNHCR.

This is the beginning of my trip and this journal. I do not know who I am writing to—myself, I guess, or to everyone, whoever you are. I am not writing for the person who may read these pages but for the people I will be writing about. I honestly want to help. I don't believe I am different from other people. I think we all want justice and equality. We all want a chance for a life with meaning. All of us would like to believe that if we were in a bad situation someone would help us. I don't know what I will accomplish on this trip. All I do know is that while I was learning more and more every day about the world and about other countries as well as my own, I realized how much I didn't know.[8]

On her first UNHCR goodwill trip to Sierra Leone and Tanzania, Jolie left the United States on February 20, 2001, arriving in the Ivory Coast the next day. For her first two days she met with UNHCR personnel and other officials, to prepare herself for her journey to Sierra Leone and Tanzania. Finally, with her own assigned security guard, she was allowed to move on, to visit camps filled with refugees from the region's wars and famine and to learn for herself what the problems were and what she could do to help.

It was a transforming experience, seeing people living in camps, owning nothing, barely surviving, yet still smiling and positive and happy to see her, happy to see anyone who would come to visit them. She wrote in her journal:

The children here grab your hands and walk with you, smiling and singing. They have nothing. They are wearing ripped clothes and they are smiling. . . . They are so happy to have what little they have now. They are no longer alone or in fear for their safety. Most of them had to walk many, many miles for days with no food or water.[9]

Being among people with nothing, Jolie felt extremely self-conscious about what she did have and stripped herself of anything of value—not just jewelry but even any clothes that looked as if they might be expensive. "I did not want to flash anything of value," she said, "not because I feared theft, but because I felt bad. I walked around people who were living with so little."[10]

At least initially, being among the refugees made her reconsider her career as an actress. It seemed to her an extremely strange and meaningless life to be living while so many people were living lives like those around her. Eventually, though, she came to realize that to them her career *was* meaningless. They were not excited to be seeing Angelina Jolie, Academy Award-winning actress—they did not know that person. Instead, they were excited to see her because she arrived in a United Nations truck, bringing food and supplies to the camp, and they appreciated the fact that this beautiful woman was there to help.

For that beautiful woman, it was an entirely new experience. Instead of being treated like a movie star surrounded by assistants ready to do everything to make her life easy, she was there to help make *their* lives easier. While many stars might cringe at the idea of touching the hands of refugees who could be carrying disease, Jolie didn't give it a moment's thought. "I would rather get infected than to ever think about pulling my hands away from these little children,"[11] she said.

Jolie was there through March 9, passing out food, washing dirty plates—doing whatever she could, whatever was needed. She felt an intense emotional bond with the people she met, one she was reluctant to give up. On her flight home from Dar es Salaam, Tanzania, to London, she was still wearing the jacket she had worn throughout the trip, now filthy beyond belief. She wrote in her journal on that flight:

Suddenly, the idea of taking off this dirty jacket upsets me. It has been my blanket. I don't want to clean up or wash off this place. These three weeks have been a new world for me—a special time—

I have changed. I like who I became here. For some reason, taking off my jacket, I feel I am detaching myself from all the people—the places. . . . The boy on the dirt floor holding his legs. The eight-year-old girl with her little baby brother in her arms. The man in the amputee camp who looked into my eyes and told me his story.

The images are like a slide show, flashes of their faces, their bare feet. I am not sure what I feel. I have never felt so much. I have to sleep now. It is both easy and hard to feel guilty leaving. From this moment on—wherever I am, I will remember where they are.[12]

While Jolie might have felt an element of guilt in being rich and privileged and having the freedom and ability (unlike the residents of the refugee camps) to fly home to Hollywood, she also knew she had the ability to help in ways that others could not. Indeed, when asked once if she would give up acting to devote her life exclusively to charity work, she replied:

I would love to, but I know I am more useful as an actress. If I do a film, I am able financially to do a lot of good and bring more attention if I only spend a week in a field. That's how I am more useful. I could build a school with my bare hands over a year, or I could buy hundreds of schools. I'm just aware that I can do more with my foot in this door.[13]

Just four months later Jolie was on another mission—this time a return visit to Cambodia. In her journal, she noted her embarrassment on just how easy it had been for her to settle back into her "real" life after her experiences in Africa. As she wrote, "Maybe I think I should feel guilty for my ability to come and go from these places when others have no choice. I know one thing. I know I appreciate everything more. I am so grateful for my life."[14]

While in Cambodia, she worked with a group called Hazardous Areas Life-Support Organization (HALO Trust). HALO is not a government organization, but an NGO (nongovernment organization), whose goal is to remove the debris left behind by war, especially land mines and unexploded ordnance (weapons such as bombs, bullets, grenades, shells, etc.) that still pose an enormous threat to the civilian population.

Through HALO, Jolie had the opportunity to learn about the damage that unexploded weapons can cause as she met with people who had lost arms or legs or eyes by accidentally stepping on them. She had the opportunity to detonate a land mine on her own. She said:

> It was a great feeling because you know something like that, if HALO hadn't been there and if you weren't detonating it, that it might otherwise be hurting someone, and you are getting rid of something that could be otherwise dangerous or deadly. So it is a great feeling.[15]

On this trip, as on all her trips, Jolie did not expect or want any special treatment. She stayed in the same barracks-type housing as the other HALO workers, who were bone-tired, hot, sweaty and dirty, hungry and, due to the lack of clean drinking water, thirsty. At night, even though her makeshift bed was surrounded by mosquito netting, she was constantly bitten by spiders, leaving her feet swollen and itchy.

And there was, of course, the constant and very real fear of stepping on a land mine. There were no bathrooms in the barracks, so like everyone else, workers and refugees alike, she had to use bushes outdoors, leaving open the very real possibility that in the blackness of night, she might accidentally leave the marked safe path and wander into an area filled with land mines.

But as Jolie later said:

And yet with all these complaints I have never felt so good in my life. I am tremendously honored to be with these people. I realize more every day how fortunate I have been in my life. I hope I never forget and never complain again about anything.[16]

How would it ever be possible for her to forget, how would it ever be possible for her not to want to help, to do whatever was in her power, when meeting people such as the ones she described in her journal? As she wrote:

While with CVD [Cambodian Vision in Development] I saw a blind man with only one arm. He was gardening. He motioned to his home. Another man walked up and helped to guide him. This man had both of his arms missing, but he could see. The two men were working together. The disabled and other "vulnerables" compensate for their needs by helping each other.

The man with no arms had six children, depending on him to provide for them. He speaks of how little rice he is able to plant. His face is so sweet. When he reentered this land after being a refugee—for over eight years in Thailand—he tried to start over, to build a place for his family. As he was clearing a plot of land, a land mine exploded. His son, a very little boy with big brown eyes, holds on to his father's shoulders. His father leans in and smiles. Only three of his children can go to school now. He can't afford to send them all. It costs 1,500 *riels* per month per child, which is the equivalent of thirty cents in American money.

As he continues to speak, I continue to write. I have started to focus on my notebook because I am very close to crying.[17]

It was clearly evident that Jolie was not just another Hollywood celebrity dabbling in charity work for the publicity. In August 2001 the UNHCR officially named her a goodwill ambassador, giving her activities official United Nations approval and encouraging her to continue doing what she was doing—helping refugees by distributing food, medicine, and other essential supplies, gathering information for headquarters, and using her own fame to draw the world's attention to nations and peoples in need.

UNHCR spokeswoman Tina Ghelli said, "Thanks to Angelina's involvement, UNHCR is now getting tons of inquiries from young people wanting to help the cause. She has also donated more than a million dollars, and she insists on paying for all her own expenses on all of her trips."[18] The one-time Hollywood bad girl had found what she had been looking for—a way to express herself, a way to explore the world, a way to help.

Another mission quickly followed the announcement: one to Pakistan from August 17 to 26, 2001. In 2001, after years of brutal civil war, Afghanistan was governed by the Taliban, a strict Islamic fundamentalist group. Pakistan, a neighboring Muslim country, was not nearly as strict as Afghanistan, and many people had fled the harsh Taliban rule and were living in squalid refugee camps in Pakistan. Jolie traveled there, despite the danger, to learn about conditions and see what she could do to help.

In August 2001, the Office of the United Nations High Commissioner for Refugees named Angelina Jolie an official goodwill ambassador, giving her activities official UN approval. Here, she holds her UN passport. Earlier in the year, she had visited refugee camps in Sierra Leone, Tanzania, and Cambodia.

Just two weeks after her return from Pakistan, on September 11, 2001, the United States was attacked by terrorists based in Afghanistan. The group known as al

Qaeda, led by a Saudi Arabian man known as Osama bin Laden, was living under the protection of the Taliban. Many Americans,7 reeling from the tragedy and wanting revenge for the nearly 3,000 victims of the attacks on New York City and Washington, D.C., blamed Muslims and Middle Eastern people for what had happened.

Jolie, who had just been in Pakistan and had witnessed the region's poverty firsthand, began to speak out about the need for assistance for Afghan refugees. She also made a sizable donation for Afghan relief. But with many people's emotions on edge, her offer of help to Afghan refugees, to *any* Afghans, struck some people the wrong way. As she wrote in her journal:

> In the days that followed, I received three death threats, including a phone call. The man told me he thought all Afghans should suffer for what they did in New York City and that he wished for everyone in my family to die.[19]

Despite the threats, she remained undaunted in her devotion to Afghan aid, explaining the threats by saying, "Emotions were running high. I understand that. It was a difficult time for everyone."[20]

It was a difficult time for everybody, but as passions eased, Jolie's words of compassion for Afghan refugees proved to be correct, as the United States sent troops to Afghanistan to root out al Qaeda and liberate the nation from the horrors of Taliban rule. At the same time, Jolie had moved her field of concern, at least temporarily, from the global to the personal. It was, she felt, time for her to become a mother. It was time to adopt a child. To do so, she would return to one of her favorite countries.

Mother, Goodwill Ambassador, Superstar

In September 2001, Angelina Jolie and her husband, Billy Bob Thornton, began the process of filling out adoption forms at the Immigration and Naturalization Service in Los Angeles. The couple had decided to adopt (or, at the very least, Jolie had decided to adopt and Thornton agreed to go along with her) a child from Cambodia, preferably from one of the refugee camps that Jolie had visited.

It was Cambodia that had first opened Jolie up to the world; it was Cambodia and its people that had touched Jolie and would forever have a special place in her heart. Even adopting a child wouldn't be enough to fill Jolie's enormous need to give back to the country, as she explained:

> Before I adopted . . . I decided to do something financially to help the whole orphanage. I can't bring

every kid home, but I can make sure that life is better for a big group of them. I helped to sponsor the kids that were older, who were not going to be adopted. The first time I saw a young boy who was dying, I said, "I'm going to save everybody and I'm going to solve it, let's get him airlifted out." But he was only one of 20,000 kids in that area. It's so sad.[1]

If she couldn't save everybody, she could at least do what she could. In November 2001, Jolie and Thornton traveled to Cambodia. It was the first time Thornton had accompanied his wife on one of her overseas missions, much to her disappointment. "He's never been to a refugee camp," she said. "I asked him to come, but he chose not to. You learn what a person is about by their behavior. And sometimes what they do hurts you."[2]

Once she had been approved as an adoptive parent, she decided to visit just one orphanage and leave it to chance which child she would adopt. There were 15 orphans there, all badly in need of adoption. Jolie slowly went from one child to the next, waiting to feel that connection, that feeling of rightness that would lead to her decision. She said:

It's the weirdest thing to go to an orphanage and know that you are going to be bringing a kid home with you. He was the last child I met. He was asleep and wouldn't wake up, and at first I thought there was something wrong with him. They put him in my lap, and I'd never held children, so I was scared that he wouldn't be comfortable with me, but he just stared at me for the longest time and then we relaxed and smiled at each other. He accepted me at the same time that I accepted him. He opened his eyes, and it was like he chose me.

I like to think we chose each other.[3]

The three-month-old boy's name was Rath Vibol. Jolie and Thornton were not able to bring the baby they renamed "Maddox" home with them right away. There were still medical tests to be done to prove that he was healthy, as well as a lengthy legal process necessary to protect his rights and those of his adoptive parents. There were complications in the legal process, and for a time it seemed that the adoption might not go through. But in March 2002, the head of the agency personally flew Maddox from Cambodia to the African nation of Namibia, where his new mother was filming *Beyond Borders* with Clive Owen.

Her happiness at becoming a mother, though, was soon mixed with pain as her marriage to Thornton continued to slowly unravel. Despite their decision to adopt, the two had spent much of their marriage apart—Thornton working on films and touring as a musician; Jolie working on films and frequently traveling on humanitarian missions for the United Nations. Indeed, throughout 2002, Jolie earned more than her share of frequent flier miles, going on missions on behalf of the UNHCR to Namibia, Thailand, Kenya, and Ecuador.

The trip to Ecuador (June 6–10, 2002) was the first time she was separated from her beloved Maddox. "It was ridiculous how emotional I felt kissing him good-bye. Leaving him with my mom and brother."[4] The trip, however, was an important one for her to make. A long-running conflict between leftist guerrillas and right-wing paramilitary groups as well as continuing drug wars had driven millions of Colombians from their homes, sending many of them fleeing to neighboring Ecuador.

Jolie went to learn what she could do to help and to publicize the fact that not all humanitarian and refugee crises are thousands and thousands of miles from the United States—some are much closer to home. In Ecuador she met with the refugees living in camps, grateful to have survived

Angelina Jolie strolls in Los Angeles with her newly adopted son, Maddox, in July 2002. Jolie and Billy Bob Thornton had adopted the boy in Cambodia in late 2001, but by the following year, their marriage was ending.

and to be in a place of safety for themselves and their children. "What was really shocking was that every individual person you meet will tell you that their immediate family was [affected]. . . . Somebody's child was killed, somebody's husband. Somebody was beaten."[5]

Her trip had been eye-opening, but when she returned to Los Angeles, she was faced with the end of her marriage to Thornton. He had spent almost the entire month of June on tour with his band, and for Jolie, his reluctance to spend time with her and Maddox made clear what she needed to do. She moved to a quiet home in Santa Monica to start to build a life with just her and her son. As she said:

> The last straw was when he took off to go on tour with his band rather than spend time with me and Maddox. I lost all my respect for him and saw that he just wasn't the kind of man I needed or wanted to be with. . . . I began to realize he wasn't willing to take the responsibility of helping me raise Maddox. I was disappointed and disillusioned.[6]

They soon began divorce proceedings, and both Jolie and Thornton went to work having the tattoos of each other's names removed from their bodies. Thornton had "Angelina" shortened to "Angel" and had the remaining space filled in with a picture of an angel. Jolie, on the other hand, underwent a series of painful laser surgeries to have Thornton's name permanently removed, saying afterward, "I'll never get a man's name tattooed on my body again."[7] On March 27, 2003, the Jolie-Thornton marriage was officially over.

She was now a single mother with a son to raise, but she was confident that she could do a good job on her own. "Maddox is going to be a fortunate kid—he's going to have a great education and he's going to travel the world."[8] Maddox was now the center of her world and the only man in her life. It was obvious that the next man Jolie would get involved with would also have to be willing to be a father to Maddox.

TROUBLES WITH FATHER

At the same time, Jolie was having problems with her own father. For years their relationship had been distant but polite. Jon Voight's behavior, though, was becoming noticeably eccentric and had begun to affect his relationship with his daughter. Communication between the two had been minimal, so to reach Jolie, Voight hand-delivered a letter telling her first of all that he did not approve of her traveling to some of the world's most dangerous places. Jolie might have been able to understand that, but she later noted that her father "said some very ugly things to me about what I was like as a person and how I was conducting my life."[9]

With that, Jolie, supported by her mother and her brother, decided to cut her father out of her life. Unable to reach his daughter on his own, on August 2, 2002, a visibly distraught Voight appeared on the TV show *Access Hollywood*, and in an emotional, tearful interview, spoke of his concerns for her mental well-being:

> I don't know what else to do. I'm brokenhearted because I've been trying to reach my daughter and get her help and I have failed. I'm sorry, really, I haven't come forward and addressed the serious mental problems she has spoken about so candidly to the press over the years. But I've tried behind the scenes in every way. I've seen Angie in tremendous pain. She carries tremendous pain. I've seen that pain on her face. They're very serious symptoms of a real problem . . . real illness. . . . My daughter doesn't want to see me because I made it very clear to her what the situation is and the help she needs.[10]

Jolie, naturally, was furious. Here was her father, who had been largely absent in her teenage years when she actually needed him, appearing on a tabloid television program claiming she was mentally ill. It was the last straw. While she did not speak to reporters immediately, she did issue a public statement addressing the issue:

> I don't want to make public the reasons for my bad relationship with my father. I will say only that, like every child, Jamie and I would have loved to have had a warm and loving relationship with our dad. After all these years, I have determined that it is not healthy for me to be around my father, especially now that I am responsible for my own child.[11]

She later elaborated by saying that what her father had done was unforgivable, adding that "I need to stay very positive in my life, get as much accomplished, do as much as I can to be a good parent."[12]

KEEPING A BUSY SCHEDULE

Jolie's life revolved around her work, her humanitarian efforts, and her son. There were movies to be made, including *Lara Croft Tomb Raider: The Cradle of Life*, the long-awaited sequel to *Lara Croft: Tomb Raider*. But perhaps more importantly to Jolie, she had missions to go on for the UNHCR, visiting places that few other people dared to go.

During Christmas week of 2002, Jolie traveled to southeastern Europe to Kosovo, a region of Serbia that was struggling to achieve independence. It was far too dangerous a place to bring Maddox, who was left at home with a nanny. Jolie wrote, "I'm sure when he is older he will understand."[13]

She spent much of her time speaking to refugees, gaining first-hand knowledge of the long-running war between the people of Kosovo and Serbia, including the everyday nightmare of being forced to live through car-bomb attacks and land-mine explosions. She described the conditions that the people were living under. "The air is so clear it is very cold. You realized it after a while, and wonder how they live in it. Most windows are broken, and many of the houses have no roofs."[14]

Again, by working to help others, Jolie discovered that she was helping herself as well. "I would never complain about the stupid things I used to complain about, or not realize on a daily basis how lucky I am to have a roof over my head and enough food to eat and that my son is healthy."[15]

Her hectic travel schedule continued throughout 2003. In the spring she traveled on behalf of UNHCR to Sri Lanka, a teardrop-shaped island nation just south of India in the Indian Ocean. Like Kosovo and so many other nations, Sri Lanka had been torn apart by a long-running civil war, resulting in a landscape riddled with land mines and other unexploded weapons and devices. Many of the nation's residents lived in abject poverty, with limited access to food and water.

Jolie traveled into the heart of the country to see the conditions and meet the people herself. At one point, she visited a house to which three generations of a family had just returned after being displaced for seven long years.

At least that family was still together. Jolie also visited a home for orphaned and abandoned girls, where more than 500 children ages 1 to 16 lived. But again, as if being orphaned or abandoned wasn't bad enough, the girls lived under the constant threat of stepping on land mines. Jolie wrote in her journal:

IN HER OWN WORDS

In her journal, Angelina Jolie wrote about the people she met in Sri Lanka:

> On our first stop we visit a returning family of three generations. They started returning about 12 months ago. We walk into the house that is right behind a large bomb crater, which is now filling up with garbage. The grandparents meet us, and three little kids run up. Neill explains that he has brought me here to show me what it is like returning home. This was the home the grandfather was born in. They left when the bombing started, and for seven years they were displaced.
>
> I look at the house and there is no roof, a broken water well, and big holes from bombs and shells in all walls. This small building houses eight people living in three rooms. I would guess that each is 10 x 5 feet (3 x 1.5 meters) wide, all with holes and bars on windows.
>
> The grandfather points to a large pile of rubble and says, "My brother's house. He has not seen it yet." He jokes, "Much work to do." There is nothing to do but cry and start all over. Another lady comes out with a very small baby. The home is on the coast, and the son has gone fishing. They were recently able to acquire a wooden boat, which is clearly a very big deal. It is a true source of pride. They have nothing but each other, but they are alive and so they are happy.*

* "Angelina Jolie's Sri Lanka Journal," April 14–15, 2003. United Nations High Commissioner for Refugees Web site. http://www.unhcr.org/4a07efbe6.html.

We walk to visit the babies and toddlers. "Don't go off the path," I am told. "It's not de-mined yet." My god, just a few feet away from all these children, there are land mines. It makes me so angry.[16]

The release of *Lara Croft Tomb Raider: The Cradle of Life* came on July 25, 2003. As with the original, the critics were not exactly kind (one wrote that the only reason it had to exist was because the first film had made money), but audiences were once again eager to see Jolie in full-on glamorous action hero mode. The film, which cost $95 million to make, earned back more than $156 million worldwide.

While Jolie was pleased with the film and its popularity, she never stopped traveling. Her next destination was Russia, which was in the midst of suppressing an uprising in its own republic of Chechnya. Russia insists that Chechnya remain a part of Russia. Chechnya, with a largely Muslim population that is very different from the rest of Russia, had declared its independence. Upward of 160,000 Chechens died in the resulting series of wars.

Jolie met with Russian government officials as well as Chechen civilians in an attempt to learn both sides of the story. Again on the trip home, she wrestled with feelings of guilt, knowing that she could pick up and leave anytime and return to her luxurious movie-star lifestyle, while those she had visited were trapped in an existence they had little control over and no escape from.

October 24 saw the release of Jolie's film *Beyond Borders*, costarring Clive Owen. The film was important to her. In it, she played a naïve American socialite who, because of her involvement with humanitarian doctor Nick Callahan (played by Owen), traveled to Ethiopia, discovered the harsh realities of a world outside her own, and eventually, like Jolie herself, went to work for the UNHCR.

The film's earnestness, though, worked against it being an entertaining movie. Critics by and large hated the film, finding it preachy and boring. Even worse, for the first time in her career, critics were displeased with Jolie's performance; the word "wooden" was used often in their reviews. It was a major disappointment for Jolie, who had worked hard behind the scenes to ensure that the film was made. But as critic George Thomas noted, "Jolie's personal interest in humanitarian causes has been well documented. Here, she shows precisely why you should never mix your work with your personal crusades."[17]

If critics didn't like her performance as an aspiring humanitarian on-screen, her real-life humanitarian efforts were receiving rave reviews. She published a book based on her journals from her first four trips for the UNHCR, simply titled *Notes from My Travels*. In the book's foreword, Ruud Lubbers, the United Nations High Commissioner for Refugees, wrote in praise of Jolie:

> Since her appointment as a goodwill ambassador, Angelina has more than fulfilled my expectations. She has proven to be a close partner and a genuine colleague in our efforts to find solutions for the world's refugees. Above all, she has helped to make the tragedy of refugees real to everyone who will listen. Angelina's interest in helping refugees, her personal generosity, and her truly compassionate spirit are an inspiration to us all.[18]

Later that year, on October 23, she was again honored by the United Nations. She received the first-ever Citizen of the World Award from the United Nations Correspondents Association, given for her efforts "to bring public attention to the plight of refugees across the globe, so that the world community will take action to help them."[19] Jolie was proud

Angelina Jolie received the inaugural Citizen of the World Award from the United Nations Correspondents Association during a ceremony in October 2003. Presenting her with the award were Nane Annan, the wife of UN secretary-general Kofi Annan, and Anthony Jenkins, president of the correspondents association.

that her efforts had been recognized: "It means that I've done good work for an organization that I care a great deal about and that I didn't let it down. If I die tomorrow I can leave my son something that says I did something good with my life."[20]

Not content to rest on her laurels, Jolie continued her tireless efforts on behalf of refugees around the world, giving generously not only of her time and energy, but of her money as well. She donated money to a children's hospital in Liverpool, England, where Maddox had been treated after a run-in with a hot tea kettle while Jolie was making a film. She also donated $500,000 to the new National Center for Refugee and Immigrant Children. By 2003, she had donated a total of more than $3 million to the UNHCR.

And she continued her travels, visiting camps set up by the Jordanian government to help care for Iraqi refugees, mainly Palestinians, who had been forced to flee when the Iraq war started simply because they were not ethnic Iraqis. The conditions there were not the best—freezing cold at night, with only the most basic necessities available.

In April 2004 she traveled on a mission to help publicize the fact that refugee camps exist in the United States as well. Jolie went to Arizona, where three such camps had been set up for people seeking permanent asylum in the United States. Every year, thousands of refugees leave dangerous situations in their own lands for the safe haven that the United States can provide. Shockingly, more than 6,000 refugees who came to the United States in 2004 were children.

The U.S. agency called the Office of Refugee Resettlement shares responsibility for the children in these camps with the UNHCR. The camps in the United States, though, are luxurious compared with refugee camps elsewhere—the children live in dorms, and the opportunity to

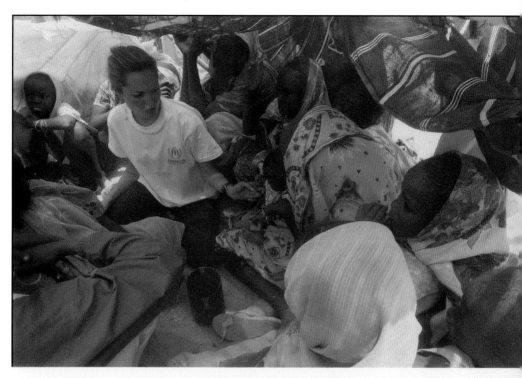

In June 2004, Angelina Jolie traveled to Tine, Chad, where she spoke with a group of Sudanese women who had just crossed the border after fleeing the fighting in the Darfur region of Sudan. Four months later, Jolie returned to the region and visited Darfur itself.

learn skills and crafts is available. Jolie noted that "these children are survivors. I am awed by their spirit and inspired by their resilience."[21]

The year 2004 was one of the busiest of her life. The full-time mother to Maddox, she also completed five films, and in addition to traveling to Arizona, made three other journeys. The most important of these was to the western part of the African nation of Sudan known as Darfur. Many Darfurians, mainly black Africans, have been the victims of a horrific genocide ordered by the government of Sudan. The Sudanese militias, known as the Janjaweed, are mainly of Arabic descent and have inflicted endless misery on the people of Darfur, raping and murdering indiscriminately in an attempt to drive the people from their own land.

In 2004, there were an estimated 1.6 million displaced people from Darfur, and more than 150,000 had been able to escape to the neighboring nation of Chad, where they huddled in makeshift refugee camps. Jolie went to work there, listening to their stories, helping newly arrived refugees to load their few belongings onto trucks for the journey to the camp, serving food, and helping to weigh and measure children during their medical exams to check for malnourishment.

So grave was the need for assistance that she returned to the region again in October, this time going into Darfur itself. After seeing and hearing for herself the horror being inflicted upon the people by the Janjaweed, Jolie used the power of her fame and celebrity by holding a press conference to focus the world's attention on what was happening to the people there and plead for additional funds to be made available to the UNHCR to protect and aid the refugees from Darfur.

Her last trips in 2004 were to Thailand and Lebanon. All of her traveling takes a lot of money, but as Jolie has pointed out, being a highly paid movie star gives her an opportunity that most don't have: the ability to put her money where her mouth is:

> I'm able to take the money and see a hospital built or build a well somewhere. So now when I return [to Hollywood] I'm half working for my family and my son, and half working to send it back into places. It makes me all that more eager to go to work and be successful because I know I can do good things.[22]

The films that she appeared in during 2004 that helped her do such good things ranged from the historical epic *Alexander*,

Oliver Stone's three-hour look at the life of Alexander the Great, to the animated feature *Shark Tale*. There was also *Taking Lives*, in which she played an FBI profiler in search of a serial killer; a cameo role in the psychological drama *The Fever*; and the role of the eye patch-wearing British commanding officer in the nostalgic look at 1930s science-fiction serials, *Sky Captain and the World of Tomorrow*.

With the exception of *Shark Tale*, in which Jolie was the voice of a glamorous fish named Lola who tries to steal the film's fish hero, voiced by Will Smith, from his girlfriend, her films failed to gain much of an audience. *Alexander*, in particular, which had been expected to be a box-office blockbuster, was a major disappointment critically and commercially. The film cost more than $155 million to make but earned only $34 million in the United States.

So while her career as a humanitarian was going strong and she was still a regular feature in the tabloids, linked romantically with every male star she made a film with (Colin Farrell in *Alexander* received much notoriety), her film career itself seemed to be stalling out. Her next project, though, filmed in 2004 but not released until 2005, would not only be her first smash hit in years, but it would also introduce her to the man with whom she'd become known worldwide as Brangelina.

Falling in Love with Mr. Smith

The film, directed by Doug Liman, was titled *Mr. and Mrs. Smith*. In it, Angelina Jolie plays Jane Smith, married to John Smith, played by Brad Pitt. Outside of the fact that Mr. and Mrs. Smith are one of the most outrageously attractive couples to ever be portrayed in a film, they are, at least on the surface, an average couple. As the movie unfolds, though, they learn that they are both professional assassins, each hired to kill the other.

The film, a potent mix of action, drama, and comedy, had plenty to recommend it to movie audiences. In some ways, though, what happens on screen pales in comparison to the real-life drama that took place behind the scenes. It was that story, which made headlines around the world, that helped turn *Mr. and Mrs. Smith* into one of the biggest hits of both stars' careers.

That story began in November 2003, when Jolie and Pitt shot their first scene together, a moment, as Andrew Morton describes it, that is now a part of Hollywood lore. In the scene being filmed, the fictional Mr. and Mrs. Smith are seen in marriage counseling. Oddly enough, for such a seemingly intimate scene, it was one of the first times the actors had actually met. It was a risk for the director to start shooting with a scene so dependent on the interaction between two actors, but he was willing to take the chance. "It was going to be rolling the dice," Liman said, adding:

> I decided I would take advantage of the awkward-ness. They don't really know each other. They're not comfortable. Just sit them down, day one, first thing in the morning, and roll the camera. You can see right then and there, they had great chemistry.[1]

The chemistry was apparent on the screen and in real life. The two actors quickly bonded as they practiced learn-ing how to shoot for their roles as assassins. "We would go to rifle ranges and actually compete with each other," Jolie said. "It made us trust each other quickly."[2] Between scenes and rehearsals, the two actors relaxed together with Jolie's son, Maddox, on a patio that Pitt had set up outside his trailer. Watching Pitt joyfully play and bond with Maddox confirmed to Jolie something that she and Pitt had known the moment they shot that first fateful scene—the two were falling in love.

Jolie swore when she divorced Billy Bob Thornton that the next man she fell in love with would have to be a good father to her son as well. With Pitt, she felt she had found him. As she said:

> I know if I ever saw a man be great with my child, that would be it for me. I ended up falling in love with a

man who I think was destined to have children and suddenly one day it felt right and there it was.[3]

Based on Jolie's romantic history, it was a most unlikely love affair. She had usually fallen for the "bad boy" type—Pitt, the Hollywood golden boy known for his acting ability (proven in films ranging from *Thelma and Louise* and *Fight Club* to *Ocean's Eleven* and *Interview with the Vampire: The Vampire Chronicles*) and his extraordinary good looks (he had twice been named *People* magazine's "sexiest man alive,"), looked like the perfect all-American guy. There was one hitch in the new relationship: Pitt was a married man.

Not just a married man, but one-half of one of Hollywood's power couples. Pitt was married to actress Jennifer Aniston, best known at the time for playing Rachel in the hit television comedy *Friends*. The couple, married since 2000, seemed, at least to the public who eagerly read about them in magazines and newspapers, to have it all: talent, good looks, and happiness. They were America's sweethearts.

Of course, what the public sees and what happens behind closed doors can be two different things, and the truth about the marriage between Pitt and Aniston is really known only to them. But what the public soon saw, during the months of filming *Mr. and Mrs. Smith*, was that Jolie and Pitt seemed to be spending a great deal of time with each other. Rumors began to quickly spread that their relationship had moved from one that was professional to one that was becoming very personal.

Asked about the rumors by entertainment reporters, the two denied that there was a relationship—Jolie told reporters that she and Pitt were just friends, while Pitt maintained that he was happily married to Aniston. But the relationship that Jolie and Pitt hoped to keep secret refused to stay that way. Photos of the couple appeared regularly in tabloid

The sparks flew from the very first moment on the set of *Mr. and Mrs. Smith*, an action film in which Angelina Jolie and Brad Pitt played married assassins hired to kill each other. During filming, rumors began to circulate that Jolie and Pitt were falling in love.

publications, and some people working on the film began to whisper to reporters that the couple had, in fact, fallen deeply in love.

That *something* was going on became apparent in January 2005, when Aniston announced that she was separating from Pitt. Jolie and Pitt continued to protest that theirs was just a friendship and nothing more. But when Aniston filed for divorce in March 2005 and one month later photos appeared of Jolie, Pitt, and Maddox happily playing together on Diani Beach on the south coast of Kenya, the relationship was out in the open. The couple quickly became a regular tabloid feature, known to the world as "Brangelina" (a name combining, naturally, Brad and Angelina).

Many who admired Jolie's work as an actor and as a humanitarian took a negative view of her role in the breakup of Pitt and Aniston's marriage, blaming her for "stealing" Brad from Jennifer. It was a true tabloid war— Hollywood "bad girl" Angelina Jolie battling it out with America's television sweetheart Jennifer Aniston for Brad Pitt. Even clothing stores got into the act, selling "Team Aniston" and "Team Jolie" T-shirts as quickly as they could make them. Perhaps not surprisingly, it is said that "Team Aniston" T-shirts outsold "Team Jolie" T-shirts by a margin of 25 to 1.

But soon the dust settled. *Mr. and Mrs. Smith* premiered on June 12, 2005, opening to critical raves and long lines at the box office, ultimately grossing close to $200 million in the United States alone, as fans as well as the merely curious flocked to see the film in which Jolie and Pitt fell in love. Aniston's divorce from Pitt became final on October 5, 2005. In the end, despite the pain of the divorce, Aniston remained positive (at least publicly) about her time with Pitt:

I don't regret any of that time and I'm not here to beat myself up about it. They were seven very intense years together and it was a beautiful, complicated relationship. I love Brad; I really love him. He's a fantastic man. I will love him for the rest of my life and hope that some day we will be able to be friends again.[4]

MOVING FORWARD

Through the tabloid turmoil of her new relationship with Pitt, Jolie never stopped working or traveling—all the distractions in the world were not enough to keep her from doing the things she wanted to do, that she felt she needed to do.

In May 2005, for example, Jolie returned to Pakistan to witness for herself the slow progress being made as small numbers of Afghan refugees made the trip back to their native land. Two months later, Jolie, along with Pitt, traveled to the culturally rich but deeply impoverished African nation of Ethiopia. Not necessarily, though, for the reasons one might think. Jolie, a single mother of one, was about to expand her family by one.

On July 6, Jolie officially adopted another child, an infant girl who was orphaned after her mother died of AIDS. As with Maddox, the moment she first saw the baby girl, living with her maternal grandmother and two aunts in a one-room shack with no electricity, she knew that she had met her new daughter. She named her Zahara Marley—"Zahara" being a Hebrew word meaning "flower" while "Marley" was for the legendary reggae musician Bob Marley.

Shortly after Jolie and Zahara arrived back in New York, she noticed that something was wrong with the baby. Zahara was underweight, had no interest in drinking milk, and had a fungus infection in her mouth. For some time, Jolie was afraid that Zahara would not survive. Julie Aronson, a doctor who specializes in the treatment of babies adopted from other countries, examined her and discovered that she was suffering from malnutrition and severe dehydration.

The cause was a severe salmonella infection that could easily have killed her if left untreated. Zahara spent six days in the hospital, and Jolie never left her side. Dr. Aronson said of Jolie, "She was there 24 hours a day keeping watch. She kept saying how much she admired her baby. She had so much admiration and respect for Zahara's strength."[5]

Even though her newest child was Ethiopian, and even though she traveled the world on behalf of the UNHCR, she still held a special spot in her heart for Cambodia. Not only was it the place that opened her up to the world around her, but it was also the home country of her oldest child, Maddox. Indeed, in 2003, she bought a 21-acre (8.5-hectare) piece of land deep in the Cambodian jungle, with 48 unexploded land mines on it.

Jolie, who had homes in Los Angeles and New York, as well as a $3.4 million converted farmhouse just north of London, built three simple bungalows there with hammocks for beds, only the most basic plumbing, and just one electric light per house. Her purpose was to help Maddox remain connected to his place of birth, to his country and his people. She said in an interview:

> He will have a very fortunate life, and I want him to be responsible to his country, to know his language, his people, to do something to make it better for his people. If he, at eighteen, said I don't want to go there, I would have it out with him.[6]

That same year, she created the Maddox Jolie Project (MJP). Based in Cambodia's poor northwestern region, its goals were to help preserve the nation's forests, endangered species, and freshwater ecosystems.

Because of her long-term commitment to Cambodia, King Norodom Sihamoni issued a royal decree on July 31, 2005, making Jolie a citizen of Cambodia. Mounh Sarath, the director of Cambodian Vision in Development, stated that Jolie deserved the honor "not because of the money she has given but [for] her good heart and love for the Cambodian people."[7] Not surprisingly, Jolie announced that she was "thrilled"[8] to accept the honor.

And the honors kept coming. Jolie was in the middle of filming *The Good Shepherd*, an ambitious film tracing the birth of the Central Intelligence Agency (CIA), when she took a break on October 11 to go to New York to accept one of the highest honors that anybody can receive: the United Nations Global Humanitarian Award, presented to her for her work with UNHCR and with refugees. There to honor Jolie were more than 700 diplomats, political and business leaders, and other dignitaries.

Presenting her the award, William Luers, president of UNA-USA (The United Nations Association of the United States of America), said that Jolie stood apart from most other celebrities involved in humanitarian work. He said, "She has gone to the refugee camps. She has sat with heads of state. She has personally and politically engaged in ways to better manage the problems surrounding this noble cause."[9]

In his congratulatory message, António Guterres, the United Nations High Commissioner for Refugees, pointed out that Jolie had given new meaning to the words "global humanitarian action," telling her and the audience that "the depth of your dedication and commitment inspired many others, especially in the legions of young people who admire you, to think about how they too can help to make the world a better place."[10]

GLOBAL ACTION FOR CHILDREN

Aside from her creation of the Maddox Jolie-Pitt Foundation (formerly the Maddox Jolie Project), Angelina Jolie has been instrumental in the establishment of numerous other charitable organizations; one of the most prominent is Global Action for Children, for which she also serves as honorary chairperson.

The goal of GAC is to help spread the word to communities and governments about the most effective ways to invest in children in order to achieve the best results for the smallest members of the world's family. GAC advocates in three broad areas, which it feels are vital to the growth of a child.

- **Health:** Every child, the organization believes, needs and deserves access to vaccines, good nutrition, and affordable medical treatment in order to combat malaria, pneumonia, tuberculosis, HIV/AIDS, and even diarrhea. GAC also strongly believes that medical care for mothers is just as important.

- **Education:** Vital to helping each child reach his or her potential is access to early childhood development, along with quality primary and secondary education. By educating the children of today, they are guaranteed a healthier and more prosperous life for themselves, their families, and their communities for years to come.

- **Protection:** Children in developing nations are at risk and vulnerable to dangers unimaginable in more developed nations. Besides poverty, abuse, and the death of a parent, the lack of a safety net and societal norms can leave young girls forced into marriage as early as six or seven years old and young boys abandoned and forced to live on their own. One of GAC's primary goals is to protect those young people living at risk from such dangers.

Visiting Pakistan in November 2005, Angelina Jolie climbs through wreckage in an isolated mountain area in Batangi, a month after a devastating earthquake killed 75,000 in the region. During their trip, Jolie and Brad Pitt reported on the devastation they saw and delivered food and supplies to people in need.

Receiving the award, Jolie announced to the audience, "Second to my children, spending time with refugees and other persons of need around the world has been the greatest gift."[11]

Her work continued. Jolie, this time accompanied by Pitt, returned to Pakistan over the Thanksgiving holidays. This trip was not connected to politics and refugees. A devastating earthquake had struck Pakistan on October 8, killing by official count more than 75,000 people. Traveling by chartered helicopter over lands barely accessible by roads, Jolie was shocked by what she saw. "You fly over the area and you can't believe it. . . . No one sitting at home has any idea what this really looks like. It is unbelievable. For 20 minutes we just saw one house after another broken. There is nothing standing."[12]

The couple did more than just investigate and report to the outside world on the tragedy. They also used the opportunity to deliver food to some of the hardest hit and remote areas of Pakistan, bringing badly needed supplies to people who had nothing.

It had been an extraordinary year for Jolie. It ended, perhaps fittingly that December when Pitt made a public commitment to her and her children by formally adopting them as his own. As a display of that commitment, the children's last names were legally changed to Jolie-Pitt. Angelina, Brad, Maddox, and Zahara were now a family.

ADDING ONE MORE

The Jolie-Pitt household was about to grow even larger. On January 10, 2006, while in the Dominican Republic finishing work on *The Good Shepherd*, Jolie made a surprising announcement: She and Pitt would soon be having a child of their own.

By the end of the month, pictures taken of the happy couple while on a humanitarian journey to Haiti told the whole story—Jolie, dressed in a tight T-shirt and jeans, was showing a substantial baby bump. In Haiti's capital, Port-au-Prince, Jolie and Pitt visited and showed support for musician Wyclef Jean by visiting a school that his organization, the Yele Haiti Foundation, was supporting.

Wanting to do more to help, Jolie arranged a deal with *People* magazine that allowed it to print the first photos of her pregnant in exchange for a $500,000 donation to the charity. By doing so, Jolie once again proved that she could

Brad Pitt and Angelina Jolie attended an anniversary party for musician Wyclef Jean's Yele Haiti Foundation in January 2006 in Port-au-Prince, Haiti. Jolie, who was pregnant with her and Pitt's first biological child, was beginning to show.

use the power of her celebrity, and the public's desire for information about her, to help others.

Jolie's grueling schedule grew to be too much for her. After collapsing on the set of *The Good Shepherd*, her doctors informed her that enough was enough. When filming was completed a short while later, and with no movies scheduled in the immediate future, she took a much needed break of complete rest for the first time in years.

When it came time to have the baby, the couple decided to do so in a somewhat surprising place: the African nation of Namibia. Why would they do that when they would have access to the best medical care that money could buy in the United States? Two reasons were given. One was that they would be as far away as possible from the paparazzi and gossip reporters based in Los Angeles and New York. Jolie wanted the birth to be a private family matter, not a media circus.

The other reason was her deep love and respect for Africa and its people. In April she traveled to Namibia with Pitt and the children to set up a base of operations prior to her scheduled delivery date two months later. While there, she agreed to do an interview with Ann Curry from NBC News.

In the interview, Jolie, relaxed and glowing from her pregnancy, spoke about her latest mission: to help improve the lives of 100 million children around the world who didn't have the chance to go to school, either because of war, lack of opportunity, or poverty.

The goal, she explained, is that by 2015, all children everywhere should complete at least a fifth-grade education. For Jolie, this was a matter particularly dear and personal to her—she knew that it would have been all too easy for her daughter Zahara to have been one of those growing up without an education. She told Curry:

> She's from a country where six million kids don't go
> to school every year. . . . Her mother died of AIDS,
> and they wouldn't have had any funds to send her to
> school. I just think, especially my daughter, there's
> no possible way she would have gone to school. She
> is so smart and strong. And her potential as a woman
> is great.[13]

Just as Jolie hoped that Maddox would be aware of his Cambodian roots when he grew up and feel a responsibility to that country, she also hoped that Zahara would feel the same way about her own place of birth. As Jolie said: "Hopefully, she will be active in her country and in her continent when she's older. And because she'll have a good education, she'll be able to do that much more."[14]

On May 27, 2006, Jolie gave birth to a baby girl, Shiloh Nouvel Jolie-Pitt. "Shiloh" means "peaceful one" in Hebrew, and "Nouvel" means "new" in French. Two days later, the new parents announced that they would be donating $300,000 worth of maternity ward equipment to two hospitals in Namibia.

Outside of Jolie, Pitt, and their two children, very few friends or relatives were there to celebrate Shiloh's birth. Jolie's brother, James Haven, was in attendance, as were Pitt's parents, who were flown in from their hometown of Springfield, Missouri. Jolie's mother, Marcheline, was in a hospital in Paris suffering from terminal cancer and was unable to attend. Jolie's father, Jon Voight, was not invited.

The family remained in relative seclusion in Namibia for two months, before returning home to a frenzied media circus, as news outlets fought to get the first pictures of Shiloh and her parents. Once again, Jolie decided to allow pictures to be taken for a hefty price tag, with the proceeds going directly to the charities of her choice. *People* magazine snagged the North American rights for a staggering $4.1 million, while *Hello!* magazine did the same for Europe and Asia for a rumored $3.5 million.

While the photos might have been pricey, as Rhona Mercer points out in her biography of Jolie, "the pictures certainly lived up to expectations. . . . Shiloh Nouvel was just as beautiful as the product of Brad Pitt and Angelina Jolie should be."[15] Within a period of just just over two years, Angelina Jolie and Brad Pitt had met, fallen in love, and built a family. It was obvious to all that Jolie had never been happier, and as for Pitt, he made it clear in interview after interview that meeting Jolie and building a family with her had been the best thing that had ever happened to him:

> You know, I've had my day. Having children takes the focus off of yourself which I'm absolutely grateful for. It's absolutely sublime. Whether you have them or adopt them, they're all blood. I'm so tired of thinking about myself. It's a true joy and a very profound love. . . . Having kids is the most extraordinary thing I've ever taken on.[16]

Within the next few years, the Jolie-Pitt family would grow by leaps and bounds, and the world's fascination with them would never falter.

Having
It All

They were, in fact, America's, and probably the world's, favorite celebrity couple. Every move they made was news. Every aspect of their lives together was reported on and discussed. Reporters did their best to get the couple to sit down to answer questions not only about their humanitarian causes, but their personal lives as well—lives that the two did their best to keep just that: personal.

The one question that everybody asked, that everybody wanted to know, was this: When were they going to get married? The most obvious answer was when they felt the need to. According to Jolie, that need to get married simply wasn't there. She once told a reporter:

There is nothing in the air. We'll never marry. The focus is the kids, and we are obviously extremely committed to the children and as parents together— to have a ceremony on top of it is nothing. We are legally bound to the children, not to each other, and I think that's the most important thing.[1]

There is, she later confessed, one thing that could send the reluctant couple to the altar. "I think it would be hard to

THE CHARITY WORK OF BRAD PITT

While actor Brad Pitt has long been involved with his partner Angelina Jolie's humanitarian efforts, he also has interests of his own, and like Jolie, is able to use his fame and fortune to help others in need.

Pitt, for example, has long supported the ONE campaign, an organization whose mission is to fight AIDS and poverty in the developing world. In 2005, he narrated the Public Broadcasting System (PBS) series *Rx for Survival: A Global Health Challenge*, which examined global health issues and their possible solutions. Along with fellow actors George Clooney, Matt Damon, and Don Cheadle, he is one of the founders of Not on Our Watch, an organization that aims to focus global attention and resources on stopping and preventing genocides such as the one in Darfur.

He is perhaps best known, however, for the way he uses his interest in architecture to make a difference in the United States and worldwide. He narrated the PBS series *Design e2*, which focused on global efforts to build structures that fit into their environment through the use of sustainable architecture and design.

say no to the kids," she told *Good Morning America* in 2010. So far, though, it hasn't been an issue. "They're not asking. They are very aware that nothing's missing."[2]

They were, in the eyes of many, the ideal modern family. And like families everywhere, both parents worked to earn a living. Unlike most families, though, Jolie and Pitt were often able to arrange it so that when one was working, the other would be taking time off to tend to the children. So in September 2006, the entire family flew to India, where Jolie

More important, though, has been his work here in the United States. In the aftermath of Hurricane Katrina, which laid waste to much of New Orleans in 2005, he founded the Make It Right Foundation. Its purpose was to organize New Orleans housing professionals to finance and construct 150 sustainable, yet affordable new homes in one of the areas most devastated by the storm: the Ninth Ward.

It was a complicated process, involving 13 architectural firms as well as the environmental organization Global Green USA. Many firms donated their services thanks to pleading from Pitt, who also, along with philanthropist Steve Bing, donated $5 million of his own money to help get the job done. The first six homes were completed in October 2008, and in September 2009, Pitt received an award from the U.S. Green Building Council, a nonprofit trade organization that promotes sustainability in how buildings are designed, built, and operated.

Pitt, like Jolie, has set an example for all to follow in how to use one's celebrity to help make a difference.

was making her first film since *The Good Shepherd*, titled *A Mighty Heart*. While Mom was busy on the set, Dad would be available to watch the kids.

A Mighty Heart gave Jolie her most challenging role in years, as she played Mariane Pearl. In this true story, Mariane's husband, journalist Daniel Pearl, was working in Pakistan when he was kidnapped by Islamic terrorists, targeted because he was Jewish and, so they believed, an agent of the CIA. Despite the best efforts to save him, Pearl was killed by his captors four weeks after he was kidnapped.

The murder was filmed, and footage of Pearl being brutally beheaded became a news and Internet sensation. Mariane Pearl, a journalist herself, wrote a memoir while her husband was being held prisoner and during the period immediately afterward. Published in 2003, it was titled *A Mighty Heart: The Brave Life and Death of My Husband Danny Pearl*. The role of the courageous Mariane Pearl, who went to extraordinary efforts to save her husband, seemed ideal for Jolie.

Filming took place in India, which, while it has a Muslim population, is a majority Hindu nation. It was felt that filming in predominantly Muslim Pakistan was simply too dangerous for the cast and crew. When not filming, Jolie met with refugees from Afghanistan and Burma, which is under the control of a brutal military government (these leaders call the country Myanmar). She met with two Burmese women who told her she looked like an actress. She responded by saying:

> That's why I'm in India, making a film . . . but I came up to Delhi just to visit with you. I am honored to be able to meet you. You are very strong women. You are amazing.[3]

Jolie not only met with refugees, but she also met with Indian government officials, to thank them for their

The 2007 film *A Mighty Heart* provided Angelina Jolie with her most challenging role in years. She played Mariane Pearl, whose husband, journalist Daniel Pearl, was kidnapped and murdered by Islamic terrorists in Pakistan.

longstanding tradition of hospitality to political refugees of any kind.

The trip to India was followed by a goodwill trip to the Central American nation of Costa Rica. There, on Christmas Day, instead of enjoying it with their family in one of their luxurious homes, the Jolie-Pitts spent it handing out presents to refugees. It was an ideal way to instill in their children the true spirit of Christmas.

Despite all of her years of work, the risks she had taken, and the money she donated, some naysayers still claimed that her humanitarian work was done just for the good publicity it earned her. Given the testimony of those who have witnessed her at work, though, that seems most unlikely. General Colin Powell, the former U.S. secretary of state, has said of Jolie, "She's absolutely serious. Her work with refugees is not something to decorate herself. She studies the issues."[4]

Even in a seemingly perfect life such as Jolie's, tragedy can occur. On January 27, 2007, her mother, Marcheline, died at the age of 56. Jolie and her brother, James, said in a press release to *People* magazine, "There are no words to express what an amazing woman and mother she was. She was our best friend."[5]

Jolie grieved for her loss, and moved on. She had her family, her humanitarian work, and her career to comfort her. In February, Jolie traveled to the African nation of Chad, continuing her work on behalf of refugees from Darfur. While there she wrote an op-ed piece for the *Washington Post* pointing out that, since her last visit to the area in 2004, an additional 200,000 people had died and the Janjaweed militia had driven another 2.5 million people from their homes. The situation had gotten so much worse that Jolie was told that she must remain in Chad for her own safety, because in Darfur, even humanitarian workers were not safe from attack.

She called on the International Criminal Court (ICC) to do its job and prosecute the Janjaweed and their sponsors within Sudan's government. She wrote, "What the worst people in the world fear most is justice. That's what we should deliver."[6] In the author's biographical note at the end of her editorial, there is not a word of her career as an actor. It simply stated, "The writer is a goodwill ambassador for the United Nations High Commission for Refugees."[7]

Then, just six weeks after her mother's death, with the ink barely dry on her bold editorial condemning war crimes in Darfur, Jolie made headlines once again. In the middle of March 2007, she traveled to Vietnam to adopt another child. When she left a short time later, she had with her a three-year-old boy, whom she named Pax Thien Jolie-Pitt. The name "Pax" is Latin for "peace"; "Thien" means "sky"

IN HER OWN WORDS

In 2007, while in Chad, Angelina Jolie wrote an op-ed piece about the crisis in Darfur for the *Washington Post*. Her column ended with:

> In my five years with UNHCR, I have visited more than 20 refugee camps in Sierra Leone, Congo, Kosovo, and elsewhere. I have met families uprooted by conflict and lobbied governments to help them. Years later, I have found myself at the same camps, hearing the same stories and seeing the same lack of clean water, medicine, security, and hope.
>
> It has become clear to me that there will be no enduring peace without justice. History shows that there will be another Darfur, another exodus, in a vicious cycle of bloodshed and retribution. But an international court finally exists. It will be as strong as the support we give it. This might be the moment we stop the cycle of violence and end our tolerance for crimes against humanity.
>
> What the worst people in the world fear most is justice. That's what we should deliver.*

* Angelina Jolie, "Justice for Darfur," *Washington Post*, February 28, 2007. http://www.washingtonpost.com/wp-dyn/content/article/2007/02/27/AR2007022701161.html.

in Vietnamese. (Since Vietnam does not allow unmarried couples to adopt, and Pitt was in New Orleans filming *The Curious Case of Benjamin Button*, Jolie adopted him as a single parent. Pitt officially became Pax's father after they returned to the United States.)

Not only was the family continuing to grow, but Pitt was also becoming further and further integrated into Jolie's life and humanitarian efforts. The Maddox Jolie Project changed its official name to the Maddox Jolie-Pitt Foundation. Its new goals, spelled out on the organization's Web site, indicates the widened range of its interests within Cambodia:

> MJP is committed to environmental security, cre-
> ating peace and stability in all communities by
> planning and implementing interventions that pre-
> vent negative environmental changes. Working
> with impoverished rural villagers and local govern-
> ments to alleviate food insecurities and increase
> access to basic primary healthcare and education,
> we're implementing projects that build healthy and
> vibrant communities.[8]

FINDING A BALANCE

Jolie's humanitarian efforts are an essential part of who she is, but so is being an actress. Her film *A Mighty Heart* was released on June 22, 2007, earning her some of the stron-gest reviews she had received in years. Noted film critic Roger Ebert wrote:

> Standing at the center of the story is Mariane Pearl,
> played by Angelina Jolie in a performance that is
> both physically and emotionally convincing. . . .
> Jolie's performance depends above all on inner con-
> viction; she reminds us, as we saw in some of her

earlier films like *Girl, Interrupted* (1999), that she is a skilled actress and not merely (however entertaining) a Tomb Raider.[9]

Despite the strong reviews, audiences did not turn out in droves to watch Jolie in a film that many felt would be too depressing. Her next three films, though, while not all critical successes, were box-office hits and showed off her skills in a wide range of roles. In *Beowulf*, she played the mother of the monster Grendel. In the animated feature *Kung Fu Panda*, she provided the voice of Master Tigress. And finally, in the action film *Wanted*, she played a supporting role as a mysterious secret agent sent to recruit a seemingly ordinary man to avenge his father's death. It was, however, just the sort of physical role that audiences loved to see her in, and the film earned her a People's Choice award for Favorite Female Action Star.

There were more overseas missions as well, including one to the Middle East. She went to Syria to visit refugees from the Iraq War and then crossed the border into Iraq to visit others who wanted to flee from that wartorn nation but were unable to do so. It had been a busy and fruitful year for Jolie, and she vowed to take some time off to rest and be with her family. But when legendary film director Clint Eastwood asked her to star in his next film, she could not say no.

The film was a murder thriller titled *Changeling*, based on the true story of a mother's ultimately fruitless search for her abducted son in 1920s Los Angeles. The film was, according to Jolie, her toughest challenge to date. "As a mother, it was harder for me imagining that someone was abusing my child while they were wondering why mommy wasn't coming to save them. As a mother, that's just the worst possible scenario. So the film was very, very painful."[10]

In such cases, when an actress is playing a role that strikes such a deep personal chord, she can be dependent on the film's director to help her through the process. And in contrast to his onscreen image as a tough guy, it was, according to Jolie, Eastwood on whom she relied to get through the film's toughest scenes. She said:

> There have been so many times I've worked on films that required a lot of emotion, and the director didn't understand. They'd do 10 takes in a wide shot and you're crying and crying. And then they'd do close-ups and you're still trying to emote with the same honesty. Clint doesn't exhaust you like that. He knows when to move on.[11]

Another goodwill trip to Iraq took place in February 2008. Then, in May, the world was surprised to learn that Jolie was once again expecting. On July 12, 2008, Jolie gave birth to twins, a boy, Knox Leon, and a girl, Vivienne Marcheline. This time however, the births did not take place in Africa. Instead, the twins were born in Nice, France, inspired in part by the longtime dream of Jolie's mother, Marcheline, to live there one day.

Again, Jolie and Pitt used the opportunity to raise money for humanitarian causes. Rights to publish the first photos of the twins were jointly sold to *People* and *Hello!* for a staggering $14 million—the most expensive celebrity photos ever taken, with the proceeds going directly to the Jolie-Pitt Foundation. Interestingly, according to the *New York Times*, it was Angelina Jolie, actress, mother, humanitarian, and apparently shrewd businesswoman, who personally handled the negotiations for the sale of the photographs.

Despite the pressures of being the mother of six children, Jolie continued her humanitarian travels, going to Afghanistan on October 24 and 25, just three months after the birth of the twins. At the same time, *Changeling* opened in the United States. Critical response to the film was cautiously favorable, but nearly unanimous in its praise of Jolie's performance. Stephen Whitty of the New Jersey

DID YOU KNOW?

The lives led by Angelina Jolie and Brad Pitt are much different from those led by most movie stars of their levels of glamour, fame, and prominence. Take the days leading up to the eighty-first Academy Awards ceremony, held in Hollywood, California, on February 22, 2009.

Jolie and Pitt were both up for Oscars: Jolie for her performance as a mother searching for her kidnapped son in *Changeling* and Pitt for his performance as a man who ages in reverse in *The Curious Case of Benjamin Button*. Most nominated actors would be happily participating in the whirlwind of media events, parties, and publicity in the days leading up to the award ceremony. Not Jolie and Pitt.

Shortly before the ceremony, the couple flew to the Thailand-Burma border, where they met with Rohingya refugees, a minority Muslim group denied citizenship in Burma by the nation's brutal military dictatorship. There, they heard the story of how the Thai military had seized six boats carrying Rohingya refugees attempting to land in Thailand and towed them out to sea—five of the ships subsequently sank, killing hundreds. In her role as United Nations goodwill ambassador, Jolie pleaded with authorities in Thailand to accept Muslim migrants trying to flee persecution in Burma.

Just days later, Jolie and Pitt walked down the red carpet at the Academy Awards ceremony, looking every inch the epitome of Hollywood glamour. Although both lost that night (Jolie to Kate Winslet in *The Reader* and Pitt to Sean Penn in *Milk*), it seems unlikely that, given what they had witnessed and heard just days earlier, their loss mattered to them all that much.

Star-Ledger spoke for many critics when he wrote that "this is one movie where the star really is the star. And [Jolie] delivers a performance of which any actress can be truly proud."[12]

For her work in *Changeling*, Jolie was nominated for a Golden Globe and an Academy Award for Best Actress, but lost both. Despite the losses, the combination of box-office success in films like *Wanted* and critical success in *A Mighty Heart* and *Changeling* had moved her to the top of the heap among female movie actors. At the end of 2008, she was ranked as the highest-paid female actor, earning more than $15 million per film. This alone was acknowledgment of the power that she held at the box office—when a Jolie film opens, her name alone is enough to draw audiences.

But the highest-paid female actor in the country still managed to balance her career with family and her humanitarian efforts. Among her goodwill trips in 2009 was one to Thailand to visit the thousands of refugees from Burma still forced to live in enclosed camps in Northern Thailand. Jolie was shocked to meet a 21-year-old woman who had been born in the camp, had never been out of the camp, and was now raising her own child in the same camp. Knowing there was little chance that the people would be able to return to Burma anytime soon, she called on the government of Thailand to give the refugees greater freedoms and help them to work and become self-reliant.

On World Refugee Day, June 20, 2009, Jolie drew attention to the plight of refugees by making a 30-second video that was broadcast on television around the world. In it she made the case for taking action: "Refugees are the most vulnerable people on earth. Every day they are fighting to survive. They deserve our respect."[13] Putting her money where her mouth is, that same week the Jolie-Pitt

Angelina Jolie and Brad Pitt walked out of an ice cream shop in Venice, Italy, in February 2010 with their children (*from left*) Pax, Maddox, Shiloh, and Zahara. Jolie was in Venice to shoot scenes for the thriller *The Tourist*, which was released later in 2010.

Foundation made a $1 million donation to UNHCR to help its work among refugees living in Pakistan.

And somehow, squeezed in between trips, Jolie found the time to make the movie *Salt*, a spy thriller in which Jolie plays Evelyn Salt, a CIA agent accused of being a Russian spy. The movie opened in the United States on July 23, 2010, and was another huge success, earning more than $36 million on its opening weekend alone, proving once again her enormous value at the box office.

WHAT'S NEXT

To all appearances, Jolie has it all. She has a beautiful family. She has a career that she loves. And she has the ability to use her fame to work for and bring attention to the humanitarian causes—the needs of refugees, education, and health care—that she cares so deeply about.

Her career has the potential to be whatever she wants it to be. In 2010 came the release of the thriller *The Tourist*, costarring another huge box-office attraction, Johnny Depp, for which she was nominated for a Golden Globe. She has been expanding her career by directing her first film on location in Bosnia during the fall of 2010. Other films are in the works as well, including the animated feature *Kung Fu Panda 2*. As if that's not enough, there has been talk of her playing the role that seems to many to be the one she was born to play—the Egyptian queen Cleopatra.

Of course, there is also her family, her charitable foundations, and her work with refugees. It's a full and rich life, and one a very long way from the troubled goth girl of her youth. It's been a remarkable transformation, and there is little doubt that, for as long as she cares to remain in the public eye, the public will remain fascinated by whatever she does next.

CHRONOLOGY

1975   Angelina Jolie Voight is born on June 4 in Los Angeles, California, to Marcheline Bertrand and actor Jon Voight; within a year, Voight will leave his family for another woman.

1978   Bertrand and Voight divorce. Bertrand and her children, son James and daughter Angelina, move to Palisades, New York.

1982   Angelina makes her film debut in a bit part in her father's movie *Lookin' to Get Out*.

1986   The family moves from Palisades, New York, back to Beverly Hills, California, where Angelina enrolls in the Lee Strasberg Theatre Institute.

1989   Angelina briefly drops out of Beverly Hills High School.

1990   Returns to Beverly Hills High School.

1991   Graduates at 16 from high school, gets her first modeling jobs, and appears in her first MTV video.

1993   Has first major role in a feature film, *Cyborg 2*.

1995   Appears in the films *Without Evidence* and *Hackers*.

1996   Marries costar from *Hackers*, British actor Jonny Lee Miller, in March; appears in the films *Mojave Moon*, *Love Is All There Is*, and *Foxfire*.

1997   Appears in the feature film *Playing God*; has major roles in the made-for-television films *True Women* and *George Wallace*.

1998   Receives Golden Globe and Emmy nominations for her work in *George Wallace*, winning the Golden Globe; stars in the made-for-television film *Gia* and in the feature films *Hell's Kitchen* and *Playing by Heart*.

1999   Wins the Golden Globe and the Screen Actors Guild Award for her work in *Gia*; appears in *Pushing Tin*, *The Bone Collector*, and *Girl, Interrupted*.

2000   Receives Golden Globe and Oscar nominations for her supporting role in *Girl, Interrupted*, wins both; divorces Jonny Lee Miller in April; marries actor and screenwriter Billy Bob Thornton on May 5; appears in *Gone in 60 Seconds*; while filming *Lara Croft: Tomb Raider* in Cambodia, becomes aware of the harsh living conditions of refugees there; contacts the United Nations to ask how to help and is assigned to make goodwill trips for the United Nations High Commissioner for Refugees (UNHCR).

2001   Appears in *Original Sin*; makes first goodwill trips for UNHCR to Sierra Leone and Tanzania (February), Cambodia (June and July), and Pakistan (August); in November Jolie and Thornton adopt a Cambodian infant they name Maddox.

2002   Appears in *Life or Something Like It*;
        makes goodwill trips for the UNHCR
        to Namibia (March), Thailand (May),
        Ecuador (June), Kenya (October), and
        Kosovo (December).

2003   Makes five goodwill trips: Tanzania
        (March), Sri Lanka (April), Russia
        (August), Jordan (December), and Egypt
        (December); appears in *Lara Croft Tomb
        Raider: The Cradle of Life* and *Beyond
        Borders*; *Notes from My Travels*, Jolie's
        journals from trips for the UNHCR, is
        published; divorces Thornton on May 27;
        receives Citizen of the World Award
        from the United Nations Correspondents
        Association on October 23.

2004   Provides voice for animated film *Shark
        Tale*, also appears in the live-action films
        Taking Lives, *Sky Captain and the World
        of Tomorrow*, *The Fever*, and *Alexander*;
        makes goodwill trips to Arizona (April),
        Chad (June), Thailand (October), Sudan
        (October), and Lebanon (December).

2005   Adopts Ethiopian child, Zahara Marley
        Jolie, on July 6; makes goodwill trips to
        Pakistan in May and November; costars in
        Mr. and Mrs. Smith with Brad Pitt (the two
        had fallen in love during filming); receives
        the prestigious United Nations Global
        Humanitarian Award on October 11.

2006   On May 27, Jolie gives birth to a daughter,
        Shiloh Nouvel Jolie-Pitt; appears in

The Good Shepherd; makes goodwill trips to India (November) and Costa Rica (December).

2007   Marcheline Bertrand dies on January 27; Angelina makes goodwill trips to Chad (February) and Iraq and Syria (August); along with Pitt, adopts a three-year-old boy from a Vietnamese orphanage—they name him Pax Thien Jolie-Pitt; appears in *A Mighty Heart* and *Beowulf*.

2008   Makes goodwill trips to Iraq (February) and Afghanistan (October); gives birth to twins (Knox Leon and Vivienne Marcheline) on July 12; appears in *Wanted* and does voice work in *Kung Fu Panda*; *Changeling* opens to strong reviews; Jolie receives Golden Globe and Academy Award nominations but does not win either.

2009   Makes goodwill trips to Thailand (February) and Iraq (July).

2010   Appears in *Salt* and *The Tourist*; Jolie and Pitt make a $1 million donation to earthquake relief for Haiti; directs first film, an as-yet-unnamed Bosnian love story, on location in Bosnia.

2011   Receives Golden Globe nomination for *The Tourist*, her sixth.

NOTES

CHAPTER 1

1. Brandi Thornsberry, "15 Quotes by Angelina Jolie," Associated Content, May 4, 2007, http://www. associatedcontent.com/article/233856/15_quotes_ by_angelina_jolie.html?cat=41.
2. Rhona Mercer, *Angelina Jolie: Portrait of a Superstar*. London: John Blake Publishing, 2009, p. 93.
3. Michael A. Schuman, *Angelina Jolie: Celebrity with Heart*. Berkeley Heights, N.J.: Enslow Publishers, 2010, p. 50.
4. Mercer, *Angelina Jolie*, pp. 119–120.
5. Ibid., p. 121.
6. Prairie Miller, "Angelina Jolie on Filling Lara Croft's Shoes and D-size Cups," NYRock, June 2001, http://www.nyrock.com/interviews/2001/ jolie_int.asp.
7. Andrew Morton, *Angelina: An Unauthorized Biography*. New York: St. Martin's Press, 2010, p. 200.
8. Mercer, *Angelina Jolie*, p. 135.

CHAPTER 2

1. Schuman, *Angelina Jolie*, pp. 9–10.
2. Ibid., p. 10.
3. Morton, *Angelina*, p. 20.
4. Ibid., p. 32.
5. Ibid., p. 33.
6. Mercer, *Angelina Jolie*, p. 3.
7. Ibid., p. 2.
8. Ibid., p. 2.
9. Ibid., p. 3.
10. Ibid., pp. 4–5.
11. Schuman, *Angelina Jolie*, p. 11.
12. Mercer, *Angelina Jolie*, p. 8.
13. Ibid., p. 8.

14. Ibid., pp. 8–9.
15. Ibid., p. 9.
16. Ibid., p. 9.
17. Ibid., p. 9
18. Thinkexist.com, http://thinkexist.com/quotation/ where_ever_i_am_i_always_find_myself_looking_ out/222305.html.
19. Morton, *Angelina*, p. 61.
20. Ibid., pp. 61–62.
21. Mercer, *Angelina Jolie*, p. 23.

CHAPTER 3

1. Mercer, *Angelina Jolie*, p. 11.
2. Ibid., p. 15.
3. Ibid., p. 18.
4. "Cutting," reviewed by D'Arcy Lyness, Ph.D. Kidshealth.org. March 2009, http://kidshealth.org/ teen/your_mind/mental_health/cutting.html.
5. Morton, *Angelina*, p. 75.
6. Mercer, *Angelina Jolie*, pp. 17–18.
7. Ibid., pp. 18–19.
8. Ibid., p. 19.
9. Schuman, *Angelina Jolie*, pp. 20–21.
10. Mercer, *Angelina Jolie*, p. 24.
11. Morton, *Angelina*, p. 77.
12. Ibid., p. 89.
13. Ibid., p. 89.
14. Ibid., pp. 89–90.

CHAPTER 4

1. Morton, *Angelina*, p. 87.
2. Ibid., p. 90.
3. Ibid., p. 91.
4. Ibid., p. 91.

5. Ibid., p. 91.
6. Ibid., p. 91.
7. Ibid., p. 94.
8. Mercer, *Angelina Jolie*, p. 28.
9. Ibid., p. 28.
10. Ibid., p. 28.
11. Morton, *Angelina*, p. 102.
12. Mercer, *Angelina Jolie*, p. 31.
13. Ibid., pp. 30–31.
14. Ibid., p. 32.
15. Ibid., p. 34.
16. Ibid., pp. 41–42.
17. Ibid., p. 42.
18. Schuman, *Angelina Jolie*, p. 33.
19. Ibid., p. 33.

CHAPTER 5

1. Morton, *Angelina*, p. 118.
2. Ibid., p. 118.
3. Ibid., p. 125.
4. Mercer, *Angelina Jolie*, p. 47.
5. Ibid., p. 48.
6. Schuman, *Angelina Jolie*, p. 36.
7. Morton, *Angelina*, p. 128.
8. Mercer, *Angelina Jolie*, p. 52.
9. Ibid., p. 50.
10. Ibid., p. 52.
11. Ibid., p. 52.
12. Morton, *Angelina*, p. 139.
13. Ibid., p. 139.
14. Ibid., p. 139.
15. Mercer, *Angelina Jolie*, p. 54.
16. Ibid., p. 56.
17. Ibid., p. 56.

18. Schuman, *Angelina Jolie*, p. 39.
19. Mercer, *Angelina Jolie*, p. 86.
20. Schuman, *Angelina Jolie*, p. 42.
21. Ibid., p. 42.
22. Ibid., p. 42.
23. Morton, *Angelina*, p. 150.
24. Mercer, *Angelina Jolie*, p. 66.
25. Ibid., p. 68.
26. Morton, *Angelina*, p. 155.
27. Ibid., p. 155.
28. Ibid., p. 173.
29. Ibid., p. 173.
30. Ibid., p. 184.
31. Mercer, *Angelina Jolie*, p. 98.

CHAPTER 6

1. Mercer, *Angelina Jolie*, p. 108.
2. Ibid., p. 105.
3. Schuman, *Angelina Jolie*, pp. 50–51.
4. Ibid., p. 8.
5. Ibid., p. 8.
6. Morton, *Angelina*, p. 200.
7. Ibid., p. 200.
8. Angelina Jolie, *Notes from My Travels*, New York: Pocket Books, 2003, p. 3.
9. Schuman, *Angelina Jolie*, pp. 52–53.
10. Mercer, *Angelina Jolie*, p. 140.
11. Ibid., p. 141.
12. Jolie, *Notes from My Travels*, p. 76.
13. Mercer, *Angelina Jolie*, p. 141.
14. Jolie, *Notes from My Travels*, p. 79.
15. Schuman, *Angelina Jolie*, pp. 53–54.
16. Ibid., p. 54.
17. Jolie, *Notes from My Travels*, pp. 109–110.

18. Schuman, *Angelina Jolie*, p. 55.
19. Mercer, *Angelina Jolie*, p. 145.
20. Ibid., p. 145.

CHAPTER 7

1. Mercer, *Angelina Jolie*, p. 152.
2. Ibid., p. 152.
3. Morton, *Angelina*, p. 208.
4. Jolie, *Notes from My Travels*, p. 196.
5. Schuman, *Angelina Jolie*, p. 62.
6. Mercer, *Angelina Jolie*, p. 156.
7. Ibid., p. 163.
8. Ibid., p. 159.
9. Schuman, *Angelina Jolie*, p. 62.
10. Mercer, *Angelina Jolie*, p. 195.
11. Schuman, *Angelina Jolie*, p. 63.
12. Mercer, *Angelina Jolie*, p. 196.
13. Schuman, *Angelina Jolie*, p. 65.
14. Ibid., p. 65.
15. Ibid., p. 65.
16. Ibid., p. 66.
17. Morton, *Angelina*, p. 234.
18. Jolie, *Notes from My Travels*, p. x.
19. Morton, *Angelina*, p. 234.
20. Ibid., p. 234.
21. Schuman, *Angelina Jolie*, p. 75.
22. Ibid., p. 77.

CHAPTER 8

1. Morton, *Angelina*, p. 239.
2. Ibid., p. 239.
3. Ibid., p. 245.
4. Mercer, *Angelina Jolie*, p. 252.
5. Schuman, *Angelina Jolie*, p. 86.

6. Morton, *Angelina*, p. 229.
7. Schuman, *Angelina Jolie*, p. 86.
8. Ibid., p. 86.
9. "Goodwill Ambassador Angelina Jolie Accepts Global Humanitarian Award," UNHCR Web site, October 13, 2005, http://www.unhcr.org/print/ 434e17b84.html.
10. Ibid.
11. Schuman, *Angelina Jolie*, p. 87.
12. Ibid.
13. Mercer, *Angelina Jolie*, pp. 262–263.
14. Ibid., p. 263.
15. Ibid., pp. 271–272.
16. Ibid., p. 272.

CHAPTER 9

1. Mercer, *Angelina Jolie*, pp. 273–274.
2. Tim Nudd, "Brad Pitt and Angelina Jolie Would Get Married—If the Kids Asked Them To," People.com, July 12, 2010.
3. Schuman, *Angelina Jolie*, p. 92.
4. Ibid., p. 95.
5. Ibid., p. 95.
6. Ibid., p. 96.
7. Ibid., p. 97.
8. Home page, Maddox Jolie-Pitt Foundation, http://www.mjpasia.org/index.html.
9. Schuman, *Angelina Jolie*, p. 98.
10. Ibid., p. 101.
11. Ibid., p. 101.
12. Ibid., p. 102.
13. Ibid., p. 105.

BIBLIOGRAPHY

Barnes, Brooks. "Angelina Jolie's Carefully Orchestrated Image." *New York Times*, November 20, 2008. Available online. URL: http://www.nytimes.com/2008/11/21/business/media/21angelina.html.

Connelly, Chris. "Angelina Jolie Unbound." *Marie Claire*. Available online. URL: http://www.marieclaire.com/celebrity-lifestyle/celebrities/interviews/angelina-jolie.

"Cutting," reviewed by D'Arcy Lyness, Ph.D. Kidshealth.org. March 2009. Available online. URL: http://kidshealth.org/teen/your_mind/mental_health/cutting.html.

"Goodwill Ambassador Angelina Jolie Accepts Global Humanitarian Award." United Nations High Commissioner for Refugees Web site, October 13, 2005. Available online. URL: http://www.unhcr.org/print/434e17b84.html.

Jolie, Angelina. "Angelina Jolie's Jordan Journal." December 10, 2003. United Nations High Commissioner for Refugees Web site. Available online. URL: http://www.unhcr.org/4a07ee4a6.html.

———. "Angelina Jolie's Kosovo Journal." December 24–30, 2002. United Nations High Commissioner for Refugees Web site. Available online. URL: http://www.unhcr.org/4a07effc6.html.

———. "Angelina Jolie's Sri Lanka Journal." April 14–15, 2003. United Nations High Commissioner for Refugees Web site. Available online. URL: http://www.unhcr.org/4a07efbe6.html.

———. "Justice for Darfur." *Washington Post*. February 28, 2007. Available online. URL: http://www.washingtonpost.com/wp-dyn/content/article/2007/02/27/AR2007022701161.html.

———. *Notes from My Travels: Visits with Refugees in Africa, Cambodia, Pakistan, and Ecuador.* New York: Pocket Books, 2003.

Maddox Jolie-Pitt Foundation, available online. URL: http://www.mjpasia.org/index.html.

Mercer, Rhona. *Angelina Jolie: Portrait of a Superstar.* London: John Blake Publishing, 2009.

Morton, Andrew. *Angelina: An Unauthorized Biography.* New York: St. Martin's Press, 2010.

Miller, Prairie. "Angelina Jolie on Filling Lara Croft's Shoes and D-size Cups." NYRock, June 2001. Available online. URL: http://www.nyrock.com/interviews/2001/jolie_int.asp.

Nudd, Tim. "Brad Pitt and Angelina Jolie Would Get Married—If the Kids Asked Them To." People.com. July 12, 2010. Available online. URL: http://www.people.com/people/article/0,,20401107,00.html.

Schuman, Michael A. *Angelina Jolie: Celebrity with Heart.* Berkeley Heights, N.J.: Enslow Publishers, 2010.

Swibel, Matthew. "Bad Girl Interrupted." Forbes.com. July 3, 2006. Available online. URL: http://www.msnbc.msn.com/id/13345611/ns/business-forbescom.

Thornberry, Brandi. "15 Quotes by Angelina Jolie," Associated Content. May 4, 2007. Available online. URL: http://www.associatedcontent.com/article/233856/15_quotes_by_angelina_jolie.html?cat=41.

FURTHER RESOURCES

BOOKS

Easty, Edward Dwight. *On Method Acting*. New York: Ivy Books, 1989.

Howard, Helen. *Living as a Refugee in America: Mohammed's Story*. Milwaukee, Wis.: World Almanac Library, 2005.

Kaysen, Susanna. *Girl, Interrupted*. New York: Turtle Bay Books, 1993.

Shapiro, Lawrence E. *Stopping the Pain: A Workbook for Teens Who Cut & Self-Injure*. Oakland, Calif.: Instant Help Publications, 2008.

Ung, Loung. *Lucky Child: A Daughter of Cambodia Reunites with the Sister She Left Behind*. New York: HarperCollins, 2005.

WEB SITES

Cambodia: Beauty and Darkness
http://www.mekong.net/cambodia/index.htm

The Internet Movie Database: Angelina Jolie
http://www.imdb.com/name/nm0001401

Maddox Jolie-Pitt Foundation
http://www.mjpasia.org

UNHCR—The UN Refugee Agency
http://www.unhcr.org

PICTURE CREDITS

Page

INDEX

ABOUT THE AUTHOR

DENNIS ABRAMS is the author of numerous books for Chelsea House, including biographies of Hillary Rodham Clinton, Eminem, Georgia O'Keeffe, Che Guevara, Coco Chanel, Xerxes, Ernest Gaines, and Cotton Mather, as well as history books such as *The Treaty of Nanking*. He attended Antioch College, where he majored in English and communications. A voracious reader since the age of three, Dennis lives in Houston, Texas, with his partner of 22 years, along with their three cats and their dog, Junie B.